W9-CFP-939

PROFESSOR WILLIAM BARCLAY, renowned teacher and author at the University of Glasgow, says of the BIBLE HANDBOOK:

> "This very useful book is written in language which the young learner will easily understand. It gives just the right amount of material — enough for the immediate need of the young person who consults it, but leaving him wanting more information and wishing to follow up what he has learned. No matter what a teacher's theological position might be, he would be glad to see it in the hands of young people.
>
> "The reader can imagine that some of the pronunciations in the Bible Dictionary grate on a Briton's ear! Otherwise, I commend the book with enthusiasm."

William Barclay

This handbook is a tool to help you learn more about the Bible and to find the answers to questions you may have about God's word.

Section One discusses every book of the Bible, profiles Bible heroes and heroines, and explores many Bible topics, covering in more detail some of the entries in the Bible dictionary.

Section Two is a collection of important Bible passages, to help you keep in mind the main message God has for your life.

Section Three is a Bible dictionary, with over 600 entries to help you understand and pronounce the words and ideas of the world's greatest book.

Section Four consists of full-color maps of Bible lands, to help you find your way around the land where the Bible and its people grew up.

About the authors...

Michael and Libby Weed are a husband and wife team who have produced a variety of religious literature for all ages. Dr. Weed, instructor in the Institute for Christian Studies at the University of Texas at Austin, has B.A. and M.A. degrees in Bible from Abilene Christian University, the B.D. from Austin Presbyterian Theological Seminary, and the Ph.D. in Ethics from Emory University. Mrs. Weed is an associate editor at Sweet Publishing Company and also serves as children's editor for the National Training Institute. She has the B.A. degree in Elementary Education and the M.A. in English, both from the University of Texas at Austin.

BIBLE HANDBOOK

A Guide For Basic Bible Learning

MICHAEL AND LIBBY WEED

SWEET PUBLISHING COMPANY
Austin   Texas

Copyright © 1974, 1978 by Sweet Publishing Company

10 9 8 7 6 5 4 3 2

All rights reserved. No part of this book may be reproduced by any means without permission in writing from the publisher, except for brief quotations embodied in critical articles or reviews.

LIBRARY OF CONGRESS CATALOG NUMBER: 73-91023

ISBN: Classroom Edition 8344-0101-0
Pocket Edition 8344-0102-9
Gift Edition 8344-0103-7

Acknowledgment

This commentary is based on the text of the Revised Standard Version of the Bible, copyrighted 1946, 1952 and 1971 by the Division of Christian Education, National Council of the Churches of Christ in the U.S.A., and used by permission.

Table of Contents

How to Use This Book........................... ix

PART ONE: EXPLORING THE BIBLE

1 Getting Acquainted with an Old Friend 1

    A.   First Impressions 1
    B.   Some Important Facts 2
    C.   The Languages of the Bible 4
    D.   A Word about Translation 5
    E.   The Bible in English 6

2 The Books of the Old Testament 11

    A.   Law 11
    B.   History 13
    C.   Poetry 15
    D.   Prophecy 16

3 The Books of the New Testament 21

    A.   Gospels 21
    B.   History 23
    C.   Letters 23
    D.   Prophecy 27

4 The Story of the Old Testament 29

    A.   Creation................................. 29
    B.   The Call of Abraham 32
    C.   The Exodus 34
    D.   Kingdom and Exile 36

**5 The Story of the New Testament —
Part One: The Story of Jesus** 41

    A.   The Coming of Jesus 41
    B.   The Life of Jesus........................ 43
    C.   The Cross 46
    D.   The Resurrection......................... 47
    E.   Lord and Christ 49

**6 The Story of the New Testament —
Part Two: The Story of the Early Church** 51

    A.   The Church as a New Community 52
    B.   The Universal Church 54
    C.   The Missionary Church 56
    D.   The Writings of the Church 59

7 The Authority and Inspiration of the Bible 61

    A.   How We Learn 61
    B.   Knowledge through God's Word 63
    C.   The Authority of Scripture 64
    D.   The Inspiration of Scripture 65
    E.   What the Bible's Authority and Inspiration
        Mean to Us 68

8 How to Study the Bible 71

    A.   The Importance of Bible Study 71
    B.   Some Helps in Bible Study 72
    C.   Scriptures for Specific Occasions 73

9 The Life of the Christian 75

    A.   Sin 76
    B.   Guilt.................................... 77
    C.   Forgiveness 79
    D.   Why Some Christians Drift Away from Christ 80

10 Archaeology and the Bible 83

    A.   Archaeology's Importance to the Bible 84
    B.   How Archaeological Finds Are Made 85
    C.   Some Significant Archaeological Finds 85
    D.   The Dead Sea Scrolls..................... 87

11 Great Bible Doctrines 89

    A.   Baptism 89
    B.   Christ.................................. 90
    C.   Church................................. 91
    D.   Covenant............................... 91
    E.   Creation................................ 92
    F.   Crucifixion 92
    G.   Faith................................... 92
    H.   Gospel 93
    I.   Grace 93
    J.   Holy Spirit 94
    K.   Lord's Supper 94
    L.   Love.................................... 95
    M.   Messiah 96
    N.   Prayer 96
    O.   Resurrection 96
    P.   Sin 97
    Q.   Worship 97

12   Great Men and Women of the Bible 99

    A.   Abraham 100
    B.   Joseph 101
    C.   Moses 102
    D.   Deborah 103
    E.   Ruth 104
    F.   David 105
    G.   Elijah 106
    H.   Daniel 107
    I.   Mary, Mother of Jesus 108
    J.   John the Baptist 109
    K.   The Apostle John 110
    L.   The Apostle Peter 112
    M.   Martha and Mary of Bethany 113
    N.   The Apostle Paul 114

PART TWO: IMPORTANT VERSES
FROM THE BIBLE

How to Use This Section 117

    A.   Baptism 118
    B.   Church 119
    C.   Confession 119
    D.   Faith 120
    E.   Forgiveness 121
    F.   Grace 122
    G.   Holy Spirit 122
    H.   Hope 123
    I.   Lord's Supper 124
    J.   Love 125
    K.   Obedience 126
    L.   Prayer 126
    M.   Resurrection 127
    N.   Worship 128

PART THREE: BIBLE DICTIONARY 131

PART FOUR: MAPS

A. Canaan before the Conquest. 244
B. The Twelve Tribes in Canaan. 245
C. Judah and Israel 246
D. The Assyrian Empire. 247
E. Palestine in the Time of Christ 248
F. Paul's First and Second Journeys 249
G. Paul's Third Journey and Trip to Rome. 250

How to Use This Book

This handbook is a tool to help you learn more about the Bible. It is organized to make it easy for you to find the answers to questions you may have about God's word.

Look over the Table of Contents before you try to use this handbook. It will give you an idea of the kinds of material the book contains and where they can be found.

Part One, "Exploring the Bible," discusses many topics related to the Bible and covers more deeply some things that are only briefly defined in the dictionary. Often the dictionary will refer you to these articles for deeper study.

Suppose you have looked up the word "Bible" in the Dictionary (Part Four). After the definition, you see the note: (See "The Authority of Scripture," p. 64). This is your clue that the extra effort of turning to page 64 will reward you with a fuller understanding of this important topic.

The maps can teach you quite a lot about Bible history and geography. They are often mentioned by letter-name ("Map A," etc.) in the dictionary, so that each time you look up a location you can see where it is found at the same time that you learn something about it.

Maps A, B, C, and E show you how the area of Palestine changed from the time of Moses to the time of Christ. Maps D, F, and G show you what the surrounding area was like in later Old Testament times, when the Hebrew people were greatly affected by the outside world; and in the time of the early church, when mission work caused Christianity to spread.

The dictionary is an alphabetical list of names and terms found in the Bible or often mentioned in Bible study. You will find that a pronunciation guide is given for most words. These guides break the words down into syllables and spell them in a way that helps you "see" how they are pronounced. Put the accent on the capitalized syllables. No guide is given for words or names that are very familiar (such as BREAD or MARK) or for words or names that are pronounced easily from their own spelling (such as ZIN). Sometimes in a two-word or three-word entry a pronunciation guide is given for only the one word if the others are familiar or easy (such as FEAST OF PURIM).

Abbreviations for scripture references used in this book are as follows:

OLD TESTAMENT

Gen.	Genesis	Judg.	Judges
Exod.	Exodus	Ruth	Ruth
Lev.	Leviticus	1, 2 Sam.	1, 2 Samuel
Num.	Numbers	1, 2 Kings	1, 2 Kings
Deut.	Deuteronomy	1, 2 Chron.	1, 2 Chronicles
Josh.	Joshua	Ezra	Ezra

Neh.	Nehemiah	Hos.	Hosea
Esth.	Esther	Joel	Joel
Job	Job	Amos	Amos
Ps.	Psalms	Obad.	Obadiah
Prov.	Proverbs	Jon.	Jonah
Eccles.	Ecclesiastes	Mic.	Micah
Song of Sol.	Song of Solomon	Nah.	Nahum
Isa.	Isaiah	Hab.	Habakkuk
Jer.	Jeremiah	Zeph.	Zephaniah
Lam.	Lamentations	Hag.	Haggai
Ezek.	Ezekiel	Zech.	Zechariah
Dan.	Daniel	Mal.	Malachi

NEW TESTAMENT

Matt.	Matthew	Col.	Colossians
Mark	Mark	1, 2 Thess.	1, 2 Thessalonians
Luke	Luke	1, 2 Tim.	1, 2 Timothy
John	John	Titus	Titus
Acts	Acts	Philem.	Philemon
Rom.	Romans	Heb.	Hebrews
1, 2 Cor.	1, 2 Corinthians	James	James
Gal.	Galatians	1, 2 Pet.	1, 2 Peter
Eph.	Ephesians	1, 2, 3 John	1, 2, 3 John
Phil.	Philippians	Jude	Jude

Rev.   Revelation

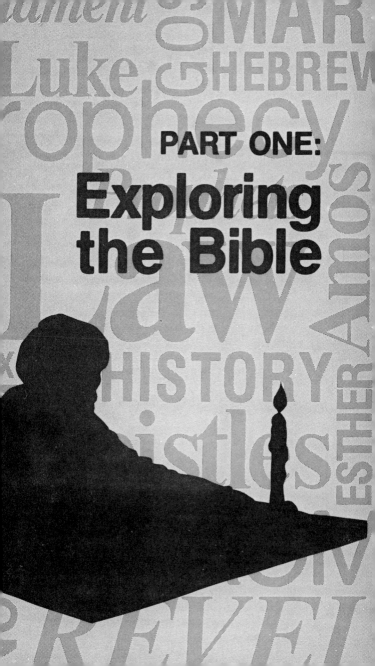

PART ONE:

Exploring
the Bible

1

GETTING ACQUAINTED
WITH AN OLD FRIEND

A. First Impressions

Have you ever thought that you knew someone pretty well and then found out later that you really didn't?

Some of you may be thinking that you are pretty familiar with the Bible and, as a matter of fact, know a good deal about it. There's a good chance, however, that there really are some very interesting and important things about the Bible which you do not know. And some of you may be like a lot of people who are frankly bored and uninterested in Bible study. There are many reasons for this, but few of them have to do with the Bible itself.

For example, when some people think of the Bible they picture in their minds a dull, black book with tiny print and no pictures. Others think of the Bible as a book that only criticizes people. But neither of these views is a fair picture of what the Bible really is.

So, before we begin, we need to examine our own attitudes

toward the Bible. Do we enjoy Bible study? If the answer is honestly "no," then we must ask ourselves why we don't enjoy it.

Two more important things should be said. First, the Bible should not be avoided or rejected just because some people misuse it. For example, a man may carelessly drive an automobile and injure a number of people. Yet this is no reason for people not to drive cars at all.

Second, the old saying, "You can't judge a book by its cover," is certainly true for the Bible. It is too bad that well-meaning people have tried to make the Bible look solemn (solid black covers) or even dainty (white covers), so that it never seems to look interesting or alive. The truth is that the Bible is as alive as the people you see every day. Its characters are not dainty. The Bible pulls no punches when it describes human activities. It doesn't try to make man appear better or worse than he really is.

B. Some Important Facts

The word *Bible* comes from the Greek word *byblos,* which referred to the inner bark of the papyrus plant. It was used to form the material for a "book" in the days when men were just beginning to make books on scrolls 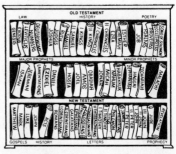 rolled on sticks. You couldn't just flip the pages but had to unwind the whole scroll—sometimes up to thirty feet! At any rate, the term *byblos* came to mean "book" and then came to refer only to the book we know as "the Bible."

The Bible is divided into the "Old Testament" and the "New Testament." The dividing point between these two sections of the Bible is the coming of Jesus. You know that we mark centuries with A.D. (an abbreviation for the Latin phrase *anno Domini*, "in the year of the Lord") and B.C. (which stands for "before Christ"). You might also say that the Old Testament is B.C. and the New Testament is A.D. The Old Testament tells the story of God's mighty acts in history among a special people, the Israelites. It takes us from the beginning—the creation—up to just a few centuries before the coming of Jesus.

The New Testament tells us of the greatest of all the astounding acts of God. It tells us of the life and teaching, the death, and the resurrection of Jesus. It tells us of the life of the early church and the spread of the gospel to all men, not just to Israelites. In a nutshell, the New Testament allows us to see more clearly the fact that men are not alone on the earth. It tells us that God has a purpose for man and that God wants man to have a full, complete, and happy life here and now, as well as in eternity.

The word "testament," which does not occur in the Old Testament and only a few times in the New Testament, means a "covenant." A covenant is an agreement between two parties. A person who enters a covenant is in a "covenant relationship," and the type of covenant will determine the type of relationship. The Old Testament (or Covenant) and the New Testament (or Covenant) describe two different types of covenants and two different types of relationships that men have with God. In Jesus Christ, men today can have a very different type of relationship with God than the Jews had under the Old Covenant. (See "Covenant" p. 91.)

C. Languages of the Bible

The Bible was written in a language very different from ours. As a matter of fact, the Bible was written in three languages, Hebrew, Aramaic, and Greek. Almost all of the Old Testament was written in Hebrew. To most of us, Hebrew is a strange language written from right to left. In addition to this, the vowels (*a, e, i, o, u* in our language) are written by using a series of dots and dashes placed under, over, and between the letters, which are all consonants. For example, if the English vowel *a* were represented by a bar (-), one would write the word *cat* as c-t or c̠t. If, in addition to this, the vowel *e* were represented by two dots below the line (¨), the word *late* would be written l̤t̠ or l̤t̠. Hebrew does this with all its vowels. The following is an example:

בְּרֵאשִׁית בָּרָא אֱלֹהִים אֵת הַשָּׁמַיִם וְאֵת הָאָרֶץ:

In the beginning created God the heavens and the earth.

Genesis 1:1

But parts of the Old Testament were written in Aramaic, a language that looks very much like Hebrew. Aramaic was probably the language Jesus spoke as a boy, and he may have even used it in teaching. There are some Aramaic parts of the New Testament still observable in the English New Testament. For example, turn to Mark 15:34 where Jesus on the cross said, "*Eloi, Eloi, lama sabachthani*" (perhaps quoting Psalm 22). Or again, look at 1 Corinthians 16:22 where one finds "*Maranatha*." This means either "come, Lord" or "our Lord comes."

Greek is the language in which most of the New Testament was written. Greek is a very complicated language which can express a wide range of ideas. It was the most widely spoken language of its day. The writers of the New Testament all wrote a kind of Greek called *Koine* (koh-i-NAY), or common Greek. It was the everyday language of the people. Like English, Greek is written from left to right. An example of New Testament Greek follows:

ὁ ἄγγελος

εἶπεν ταῖς γυναιξίν· μὴ φοβεῖσθε ὑμεῖς· οἶδα γὰρ
ὅτι Ἰησοῦν τὸν ἐσταυρωμένον ζητεῖτε· οὐκ ἔστιν
ὧδε· ἠγέρθη γὰρ καθὼς εἶπεν· δεῦτε ἴδετε τὸν
τόπον ὅπου ἔκειτο.

The angel said to the women, "Don't fear, I know that you look for Jesus who was crucified. He is not here; he has risen, as he said. Come look at the place where he lay."

Matthew 28:5-6

D. A Word about Translation

Looking at these languages, we become aware that we must have a good translation of the Bible. We must remind ourselves that we have none of the original copies of any of the biblical writings. Our earliest manuscripts go back to the second century and are only scraps or small pieces. Though important, they are certainly not enough to make a translation from. The earliest complete manuscripts go back to the fourth or fifth century—three hundred years or more after the original writing was done.

Translators are always studying and trying to get a better understanding of

Koine Greek. Sometimes archaeologists make discoveries that help them understand difficult parts. So translators continue to be more and more accurate in their understanding of the biblical languages.

But the translator's task is only half done when he understands the original language. He still has to put the ancient message into the modern language, and it is important to know how to express the original meaning. It is also necessary to recognize that our language is continually changing. So the task of translation must go on and on, since words lose or change their meaning over the years. For example, the word "awful" used to mean that something was worthy of reverence or respect. This is not what we usually mean when we speak of something being "awful" today. As words change their meanings, the translator must find the best way to express the meaning of the original language in clear, understandable terms.

E. The Bible in English

Like so many things that we are around all the time, the Bible is often taken for granted. Today, we can buy a New Testament in the drug store for less than two dollars. It is hard for us to imagine that there was a time when the Bible was not available—at any price.

Yet, compared to the amount of time that the Bible has not been readily available, it has only been for a very short time that men and women have been able to read and own a Bible.

There are many reasons for this. Before the development of the printing press, books had to be copied by hand, and this made them so expensive that only the very rich could afford them. Also, some religious authorities felt that the Bible could not be read or understood by the common man. They did all within their power to stop the free circulation of the Bible.

Many men in different lands risked their lives to translate the Bible into the language of the people so that they could read the Old and New Testaments for themselves. Two of these men, in England, were John Wycliffe and William Tyndale.

John Wycliffe is responsible for the first complete translation of the Bible into English about 1380, before the invention of the printing press. Wycliffe was unable to read Greek, so he made his translation from the Latin. The Bible had been kept in the Latin language for many centuries although few people could read it, including the

When he saw the people he went vp into a mountayne, and when he was set, his disciples came to hym, and he opened hys mouthe, and taught them saying: Blessed are the povre in sprete: for theirs is the kyngdome of heven. Blessed are they that morne: for they shalbe conforted. Blessed are the meke for they shall inheret the erth.

church officials. Wycliffe's efforts to make the Bible available to the people were strongly opposed by religious authorities.

William Tyndale is sometimes called the "father of the English Bible" because he was responsible for the first *printed* version of the New Testament in English in 1525. Tyndale's work was more careful than Wycliffe's, for Tyndale translated from the original Greek rather than from the Latin that had grown full of mistakes and errors down through centuries of copying. Nonetheless, Tyndale's work was met with anger and persecution. Copies of his book were seized and burned. Tyndale himself was burned at the stake in 1536. We are told that he died with a prayer on his lips that God would make the king of England understand the importance of letting the common people have and read the Bible.

After Tyndale, there were other efforts to translate the Bible into English and make it available to the people. It was not until 1604, however, when King James called a group of scholars to set themselves to the task of a translation from the Greek and Hebrew, that the Bible was really made available to the public. In 1611, the King James Bible was printed. The original copies included a statement from the translators defending themselves against criticism. Many people were using older translations like Tyndale's and resented the new translation.

The King James Bible has three important strengths. First, it was the work of a group of scholars using the Hebrew, Aramaic, and Greek manuscripts. It was not the work of any single man, and so it did not run the risk of reflecting just the opinions and views of a single individual.

Second, the King James Bible was in the language of the people—not the common people, but the educated people of the time. Thus it was easily understood, and made the Christian religion a thing of the present and not, like the Latin translations, just a thing of the past.

Third, the translators were aided by the efforts—both the success and the mistakes—of the men who had gone before (such as Wycliffe and Tyndale). They were also helped by the increased knowledge of the biblical languages that came with the continuing discovery of more manuscripts.

In 1870 (250 years later), it was felt that the King James Version needed revising. Another committee was selected to work at this task. These scholars had the benefit of new knowledge of the Greek and Hebrew languages that had been gained through recently-found manuscripts. Many of these manuscripts were much older than those that the translators of the King James Version had available in 1604–1611. This revision was published as the English Revised Version in 1881. In 1901, this same revision of the King James Bible was published in the United States (with minor spelling changes) and called the American Standard Version.

The Revised Standard Version, whose translators had the use of even older and better manuscripts, appeared in complete form in 1952. Since its appearance, there have been other translations by committees of scholars, perhaps the most noticeable being the New English Bible. In addition to these there have been translations by individual scholars such as J.B. Phillips.

The number of translations available to the modern Bible student is often taken as cause for alarm. Certainly if there were a number of careless and erroneous translations being sold, there would be reason for such an attitude. However, this is simply not so. No one translation is such that it may be called perfect. Translations are done by men and men make mistakes.

It is fortunate that there *are* a number of translations. By using more than one translation, the Bible student can get a pretty close understanding of the text. Also, he can clearly see where translators differ and use this to guide himself into deeper study. The important thing is not so much which translation a Bible student prefers but that he does study the Bible in a translation that he understands. Still more desirable is the use of several translations.

The following verses illustrate the type of differences and similarities that are found among different translations. All are translations of 1 Corinthians 9:25.

King James Version

And every man that striveth for the mastery is temperate in all things. Now they *do it* to obtain a corruptible crown; but we an incorruptible.

American Standard Version

And every man that striveth in the games exerciseth self-control in all things. Now they *do it* to receive a corruptible crown; but we an incorruptible.

Revised Standard Version

Every athlete exercises self-control in all things. They do it to receive a perishable wreath, but we an imperishable.

J. B. Phillips

Every competitor in athletic events goes into serious training. Athletes will take tremendous pains—for a fading crown of leaves. But our contest is for an eternal crown that will never fade.

2

THE BOOKS OF THE OLD TESTAMENT

We need to see how the books of the Bible are arranged before we look more closely at the contents of each one. Just as a newspaper contains the work of many different writers, the Bible also contains the writings of men who never knew each other, men writing about different things and at different times. The Old Testament contains many kinds of writing: historical narratives, great poetry, and songs praising God. To overlook this fact can be misleading and make the Bible hard to understand.

The thirty-nine books of the Old Testament can be divided into five different groups: Law, history, poetry, major prophets, and minor prophets.

A. Law

The Law, or Torah as the Jews called it, was believed to have been written by Moses perhaps fifteen hundred years before the time of Jesus. The Law consists of the first five books in the Old Testament and is often called the Pentateuch, which means five books or "five-fold book." The five books of the Pentateuch are Genesis, Exodus, Leviticus, Numbers, and Deuteronomy.

Genesis (JEN-eh-sis) is the first book of the whole Bible. It tells of the beginning of the universe, man, sin, and God's plan to redeem his creation. Genesis tells us about Adam and Eve, Noah and the flood, and God's calling Abraham to be his special servant. It also tells about Isaac's

A WORD FOR THE WISE

Genesis

(JEN-eh-sis), which means *beginning,* has many relatives. "Genes" are the building blocks present from the *beginning* of life. To "generate" power is to *begin* or produce it. A "genealogy" traces a family's ancestors back to the time it *began,* if possible.

son, Jacob, and his twelve sons who became fathers of the twelve tribes of Israel. Genesis ends by telling how the twelve tribes came to live in Egypt.

Exodus (EKS-oh-dus) means "to leave" and begins with Israel in Egypt but no longer welcome as visitors. The Israelites had come to be held captives as slaves. Exodus is the story of how God called Moses and his brother Aaron to the special task of leading Israel out of Egypt. After God sent several disasters (or "plagues") upon the Egyptians, their ruler (the Pharaoh) finally allowed Israel to leave Egypt. Exodus tells of God's miraculous parting of the Red Sea and Israel's journey to Mount Sinai where Moses received the Law (the Ten Commandments) and instructions for building the tabernacle.

Leviticus (leh-VIT-i-kus) is named for the tribe of Levi from which Israel's priests came. Leviticus contains instructions for Israel's priests in handling the tabernacle (the movable place of worship) and performing the various religious ceremonies and sacrifices. It has been called the "Priest's Handbook."

Numbers continues Israel's history and tells of the chosen people's reaching the promised land. Because of their lack of faith, they were made to spend forty years wandering in the wilderness before being allowed to enter the promised land.

Deuteronomy (DYOO-ter-ON-oh-mee) tells of the arrival of Israel at the Jordan River after the forty years of wandering, ready to enter the promised land. However, Moses had been told by God that he could not enter. He called representatives of the twelve tribes together and recounted their history to them. He repeated the Law, predicted their doom if they departed from God's will, and the blessings which would be theirs if they continued in the Law.

B. History

The second division of the Old Testament contains twelve books of history. These books tell of Israel's history from the time of the conquest of Canaan until the second captivity in Babylon and Israel's eventual return once again to the homeland.

Joshua (JOSH-you-uh) is named after the leader of Israel who followed Moses and led Israel in the conquest of the promised land. The book tells of the various battles of the conquest and the settlement of the tribes of Israel in the promised land. It ends with Joshua's farewell address to the tribes.

Judges tells the story of Israel's history for the next four hundred years after the conquest, when Israel was ruled by judges—leaders through whom God spoke and led his people.

Among the great judges were men like Gideon and Samson and a woman named Deborah.

Ruth is the story of a romance during the period of the judges of Israel. Ruth is named for a Moabite woman who married an Israelite. Ruth was the great-grandmother of the great king of Israel, David. She was also an ancestor of Jesus (Matt. 1:5).

First Samuel (SAM-you-el) records the change of Israel's government from a judgeship to a monarchy or kingdom. It tells how Samuel, Israel's last judge, anoints Saul, Israel's first king. The book ends with the death of Saul.

Second Samuel continues the history of Israel after Saul's death, telling of David's reign as Israel's greatest king.

First Kings begins with the reign of David's son, Solomon. It tells the story of many of Israel's kings and closes with the death of King Ahab. In 1 Kings, we read of the division of the kingdom of Israel into two rival kingdoms, Israel and Judah. We also read of some of the early prophets of Israel such as Elijah and Micaiah.

Second Kings continues the history of the two kingdoms, telling of the fall of the Northern Kingdom, Israel, in 721 B.C. It continues the history of Judah for another 120 years until its fall to Babylon in 600 B.C. In 2 Kings, we read of the great prophet Elisha, who followed Elijah.

First and Second Chronicles (KRON-i-kulz) retell the same story as 2 Samuel and 1 and 2 Kings. But where 1 and 2 Kings tell of both Northern and Southern Kingdoms, the Chronicles tell mainly of the Southern Kingdom, Judah.

Ezra (EZ-ruh) gives the history of God's people held captive in Babylon as they begin to return to Jerusalem and rebuild it after seventy years of captivity.

Nehemiah (NEE-uh-MY-uh) tells of the same period as Ezra but gives more attention to the reconstruction of the city of Jerusalem and a restoration of Israel's worship of God.

Esther (ES-ter) tells the story of a Jewish girl who, during the period of captivity, became a queen and was able to save her people from destruction by evil men. The book of Esther honors this girl and the Jews held a feast each year in her honor (called the Feast of Purim).

C. Poetry

The five books of poetry have a majestic beauty as they express prayer and praises to the Lord. They were used in religious feasts and festivals of the Jews.

Job (JOBE) is the story of a man's great suffering and deals with the question of why human beings suffer.

Psalms (SALMZ) contains 150 songs of prayer and praise to God which were written by different men, including David and Solomon. These songs were written for both private and public worship. Many of them were used in worshiping God in the Jerusalem Temple.

Proverbs (PRAH-verbz) is a collection of wise sayings most of which were written by David's son, Solomon. Proverbs has many short sayings about such practical things as self-control, laziness, cheerfulness, rearing children, and respect for God.

Ecclesiastes (eh-KLEE-zee-AS-teez) is thought to be written by Solomon, apparently near the end of his life. The writer tells us of the meaninglessness and purposelessness of life apart from trust in God. He sought satisfaction in many things but always found that nothing brings true satisfaction but God. His conclusion is that all should remember God in the days of their youth. To fear God and keep his commandments is the whole duty of man.

Song of Solomon (SAHL-oh-mun) is a love song written by Solomon. It is also called the "Song of Songs," possibly because Solomon liked it best of the 1,005 songs which he wrote. Some have thought that Solomon wrote the song in celebration of his marriage to his favorite wife.

D. Prophecy

There are seventeen prophetic books in the Old Testament. Five of these are grouped together as "major prophets." The word "major" refers to the length of the book and not to its importance. The major prophets are Isaiah, Jeremiah, Lamentations, Ezekiel, and Daniel. The twelve books of "minor prophets" are smaller only in size, not in importance. They are Hosea, Joel, Amos, Obadiah, Jonah, Micah, Nahum, Habakkuk, Zephaniah, Haggai, Zechariah, and Malachi.

Isaiah (eye-ZAY-uh) was a prophet during the reign of four different kings from about 740 to 681 B.C. Isaiah, perhaps more than any other of the prophets, looked for the coming of the Messiah and is sometimes called the "Messianic Prophet."

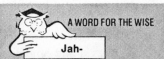

A WORD FOR THE WISE

Jah-

(yah) is short for *Jahweh* or *Jehovah*, a Hebrew name for God. You can see it in the last part of the names Isa*iah*, Jerem*iah*, and Eli*jah*, and it gives these names a special reference to God. For example:

Isaiah = Salvation of Jehovah
Elijah = Jehovah my God

Watch for *iah* and *jah* in other Bible names.

Jeremiah (JER-eh-MY-uh), a little later than Isaiah, was God's prophet when Jerusalem fell to the Chaldeans. He foresaw the defeat of Judah and its captivity. Knowing that Jerusalem could not hold out against its enemies, he advised surrender to save the city, and was branded a traitor. Like Isaiah, Jeremiah also prophesied a time when God would establish a new covenant with his people.

Lamentations (LAM-en-TAY-shunz) is a series of laments or sorrowful songs over the destruction of Jerusalem. It was written by Jeremiah soon after the city fell to Judah's attackers.

Ezekiel (ee-ZEE-kyuhl) is named after a prophet living in the exile who served from about 595 until 571 B.C. The book of Ezekiel describes the prophet's call to serve God. He prophesied the return of God's people to Jerusalem and the restoration of the Temple.

Daniel (DAN-yuhl) was also a prophet during the exile. He served as an official in the court of the Babylonian king, Nebuchadnezzar. The first half of the book of Daniel tells about the prophet's life. The second half reports four of Daniel's visions foreseeing God's ultimate victory over human history.

Hosea (ho-ZAY-uh) is named after one of the great prophets of God's people whose primary work was to call them back to God. Hosea is remembered for the love he showed for his unfaithful wife, whom he brought home after years of absence. This love is shown to be the same kind of love God shows his own unfaithful people.

Joel (JO-uhl) was written to urge God's people to repent. It looks forward to God's coming judgment and an outpouring of God's Holy Spirit on the people of all nations.

Amos (AY-mus) is remembered as the great prophet of justice. After criticizing other nations, Amos exposed the false security of God's own people. Their religion had become displeasing to God because they neglected justice and mercy. Amos foretells the coming judgment of God and future restoration of prosperity for all.

Obadiah (OH-buh-DIE-uh) is a very short book dealing primarily with the predicted destruction of the nation of Edom, a nation which was very wicked and hostile to God.

Jonah (JO-nuh) tells the well-known story of the prophet swallowed by a fish. The book emphasizes God's love for Gentiles and looks forward to the Christian mission to all men.

Micah (MY-kuh) predicts the fall of the Northern Empire, Israel. Micah is more interested, however, in the sins of the Southern Kingdom, Judah. The book looks forward to God's eventual rule.

Nahum (NAY-hum) is written in the style of a poem praising the greatness of God and predicting the downfall of Nineveh, the capital of Assyria.

Habakkuk (huh-BACK-uk) is a series of questions by its little-known writer as to why God's chosen people have become so wicked. When told that God will destroy Judah by using the Chaldeans, Habakkuk was concerned because the Chaldeans' wickedness was even greater than that of Judah. God answered Habakkuk's questions by saying that he would also destroy the Chaldeans. His own people must learn to live by trust and faith in God.

Zephaniah (ZEF-uh-NYE-uh) calls attention to a coming day when God will judge and punish the wicked of all nations, Judah included. Zephaniah looks forward to a time when God will more fully reveal himself and men of all nations will be brought to God and will praise him. Israel will be restored.

Haggai (HAG-gay-eye) contains five short messages dealing with the rebuilding of the Jerusalem Temple (520–516 B.C.).

Zechariah (ZEK-uh-RYE-uh) was written about the same time as Haggai. Zechariah recounted how God has allowed his people to suffer because of their own wickedness. He encouraged the people regarding their future. Among other things, Zechariah looked forward to the time when Jerusalem would be a great city once again, to God's coming judgment on other nations, and, finally, to God's rule over all the earth.

Malachi (MAL-uh-kye) is the last book in the Old Testament. It is strongly critical of God's people because of a general lack of interest in rebuilding the Temple and a moral and religious decline. Like so many of the prophets, Malachi also looked forward to a coming "day of the Lord," which may include the coming of Christ.

3

THE BOOKS OF THE NEW TESTAMENT

The New Testament contains twenty-seven books. Like the Old Testament, the New Testament has different kinds of writing. There are four different types of literature in the New Testament: Gospels, History, Letters, and Prophecy.

A. Gospels

The term "gospel" comes from a Greek word, *euangelion,* meaning "good news." For the early Christian, the gospel centered in the announcement of what God had done for man through Jesus Christ. In a sense, Jesus was the good news and the message about him was also the good news. In time, after the message had been written down, the written message itself was called "gospel." The New Testament contains four different books called gospels. They were written to meet the needs of the young church. As the apostles began to die and false teachers began to harm the church, it became clear that written teachings could guard the church against those who would lead others astray. Also, written teachings about

Jesus could be copied and sent to many more places than one man could visit. So the gospels came to be helpful tools in teaching non-Christians the good news.

Three of the four gospels are called "synoptic" (sin-OP-tik), meaning "seen together," because they let us see Jesus from a similar point of view. They tell us many of the same things that Jesus said and did in almost the same words. The three synoptic gospels are Matthew, Mark, and Luke.

Matthew (MATH-you) was written especially to Jewish Christians and contains five different sections of Jesus' teaching. It traces the birth-line of Jesus back to David and Abraham.

Mark is the shortest of the synoptics. It tells the story of Jesus in a brief and straightforward style, emphasizing his actions more than his words.

Luke is much like Matthew but also tells us of many things Jesus did and said on his way for the last visit to Jerusalem. It also places more emphasis on the role of certain women, such as Mary, the mother of Jesus, and Elizabeth, the mother of John the Baptist.

John is different from the synoptic gospels. John probably wrote his gospel much later than the writers of the synoptics. John's readers, therefore, may have been familiar with the synoptic gospels. From his knowledge of the many things that Jesus said and did, John carefully chose to tell some of those things not mentioned in the synoptics. He especially stressed the sayings of Jesus.

B. History

Although the gospels and other writings of the New Testament certainly have history in them, only one book of the New Testament is primarily thought of as history.

Acts, written by Luke, is the second volume of Luke's writings. Acts tells us of the fast growth of the church from the small and lonely group of disciples in the upper room in Jerusalem to the very center of the Roman Empire, the city of Rome. Luke told a story of courage and suffering. It is the story of the power of God enabling the early church to fulfill its mission of preaching the good news to all the world. The main characters in the book of Acts are the apostles and their companions, especially Peter (up to chapter 12) and Paul (from chapter 13 on). Acts helps us place many of the letters of the New Testament in their original setting.

C. Letters

Most of the letters (also called *epistles*) of the New Testament are written by the apostle Paul. There are thirteen of Paul's letters. They may be divided into three categories.

(a) *Early letters:*

1 Thessalonians	1 Corinthians	Galatians
2 Thessalonians	2 Corinthians	Romans

In these letters, Paul opposes those who distorted the meaning of the new covenant between God and man.

(b) *Prison letters:*

Philippians	Colossians
Philemon	Ephesians

These are called "prison letters" because they all seem to have been written while Paul was in prison—probably in Rome. They were written after the "early letters."

(c) *Pastoral letters:*

1 Timothy	2 Timothy	Titus

Paul's last letters are called "pastoral letters" because they deal with specific needs in "tending the flock," or caring for the needs of the church.

In addition to Paul's thirteen letters, the New Testament contains eight others by various authors. These are usually called the general letters, and they include:

Hebrews	1 Peter	1 John	3 John
James	2 Peter	2 John	Jude

We will take a brief look at the contents of all these letters, considering them in the order in which they appear in the New Testament (except for Jude—p. 26).

Romans (RO-munz) was written to Christians Paul had never met. It addresses many of the problems they had in understanding the new covenant of man with God. It is in many ways a sort of introduction to Paul's entire thought.

First and Second Corinthians (kor-IN-thee-unz) responded to questions from Christians in the city of Corinth. Paul wrote regarding such things as marriage, the Lord's Supper, spiritual gifts, and the resurrection.

Galatians (guh-LAY-shunz) was written to Christians in Galatia who were in danger of losing Christ and going back under the law of Moses.

Ephesians (eh-FEE-zhunz) was addressed to Christians at Ephesus but was probably also intended to be circulated among other churches. In Ephesians, Paul told how God had torn down the divisions between Jews and Gentiles. He stressed the unity of the church and her task in the world.

Philippians (fuh-LIP-ee-unz) was written to thank Christians at Philippi for sending help to Paul. It also emphasizes the privileges of suffering for the cause of Christianity and warns against false teachers.

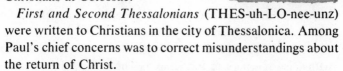

Colossians (kuh-LAH-shunz) stresses what Christ has done and the fact that Christians need not fear any other powers or worship any other imaginary gods. It was written to Christians at Colossae.

First and Second Thessalonians (THES-uh-LO-nee-unz) were written to Christians in the city of Thessalonica. Among Paul's chief concerns was to correct misunderstandings about the return of Christ.

First and Second Timothy (TIM-oh-thee) were written by Paul to his young co-worker and brother in Christ, Timothy. They were written toward the end of Paul's life and contain many personal messages as well as discussions about the administration of church life.

Titus (TIE-tus) was another Christian brother to whom Paul wrote during the latter part of his life. This letter also deals with concerns of church life as well as individual conduct.

Philemon (fuh-LEE-mun) is the name of the owner of a runaway slave. Paul had met and converted the slave and was sending him back to his master with this letter addressed to Philemon. Paul encouraged Philemon to receive his slave as a Christian brother.

Hebrews (HEE-brooz) reads much like a sermon. It addresses Christians who are in danger of growing so uninterested in their faith that they just drift away. The writer encouraged them to renew their faith and commitment. The writer of Hebrews is unknown. Some have suggested Apollos and many believe that the letter may have been written by Paul.

James is a short letter of only five chapters that read much like a sermon. The writer (possibly the brother of Jesus) stressed the importance of resisting temptation, the need to express faith in outward deeds, the evil use of the tongue, and the sin of discriminating against the poor.

First Peter was written to Christians living in a world that was growing more and more hostile. Peter told Christians to keep high the hope that they have in Jesus because of his resurrection. The last chapter calls on elders of the church to lead by example, and with humility.

Second Peter and *Jude* are quite similar. Both are concerned with false teachers in the church. The main point of these letters is to "hold fast" and not be tricked into believing some un-Christian teaching.

First, Second, and *Third John* are some of the most interesting and inspiring writings in the New Testament. They were written by the same person who wrote the gospel of John and Revelation. There is a strong emphasis on love in these letters, but they also contain forceful attacks against false teachers. They tell us bluntly that one who claims to "know God" but does not live in a loving manner with his fellowmen is a liar. John says that our lives must prove our belief in God.

D. Prophecy

The New Testament contains only one book of prophecy.

Revelation (REV-eh-LAY-shun) is an entirely different kind of writing from the other writings in the New Testament. It is filled with strange symbols and word pictures. If you compare it with parts of the Old Testament books of Daniel and Ezekiel, you will see similar points. The book was written to churches facing great persecution. The writer assured his readers that in spite of the way things seem to be going, God would be victorious in the struggles then going on. Revelation encourages Christians not to lose hope and to calmly await Christ's final victory.

4

THE STORY OF THE OLD TESTAMENT

In the Old Testament, a book of over a thousand pages in today's Bibles, four events stand out as most important: (a) the creation, (b) the call of Abraham, (c) the exodus from Egypt, and (d) the kingdom and the exile.

The Old Testament is mostly the story of how God met certain people in history—that is, in their day-to-day life. It is the story of how God called the Israelite nation to be his own people. It is the story of how God revealed his purpose for man in great events in history.

A. Creation

The first book of the Bible, Genesis, begins with the story of the creation of all things. The Bible simply states that God brought things into being—we really do not have a "play by play" description of it. The writer of Hebrews says it is something we accept *by faith:* "By faith we understand that the world was created by the word of God, so that what is seen was made out of things which do not appear" (Heb. 11:1).

Other views. The faith that God created the world from nothing prevented Israel from falling into several false views of creation. One of these is *pantheism.* This is the belief that God is found in mountains, trees, and all creation.

The Genesis account of creation clearly refutes pantheism. It tells us that God is separate from the creation, not a part of it. It tells us that God brought the creation into being and that he exists apart from it. This view generally saved God's people from such superstitions as the belief that an idol or grove of trees was holy because God actually lived in them.

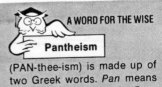

A WORD FOR THE WISE

Pantheism

(PAN-thee-ism) is made up of two Greek words. *Pan* means "all" or "every" (as in *Pan-American*, referring to all the Americas). *Theos* means "God," as in *theology*, the study of God. Hence, *pan + theism = all-is-God*, or the belief that God dwells in everything.

The creation account also opposes *dualism*, a view that there is a good god and an evil god who are always warring with each other. Sometimes dualists have called the good principle "spirit" and the bad principle "matter." If a person held this view, he would believe that the world is evil because it is made of matter, which itself is evil.

But Genesis will not let us be dualists. It tells us there is only one God, and he is the Creator of all—the material as well as the spiritual world. Furthermore, several times in the first chapter of Genesis we are told that God's creation is good. "Matter" therefore, cannot of itself be evil. In the story of the Fall, also in Genesis (ch. 3), we discover that the source of sin is man's own selfishness. The Bible just won't let us blame sin on God's creation.

Man's task. In addition to telling us how God is related to the world, the creation account tells us how *man* should relate to the world. He is to be a *steward*—that is, he is to use and manage the universe for its owner, God. The command to the first man was:

> Be fruitful and multiply, and fill the earth and sub-due it; and have dominion over the fish of the sea and over the birds of the air and over every living thing that moves upon the earth.

> Genesis 1:28

When man masters the seas, spans the continents, and even steps out on the moon, he is fulfilling his God-given task of "subduing" the earth. The world is made for men, and is to be used for man's good. There is a place for the scientist, the doctor, engineer, and farmer in these opening words of the Bible.

But we must avoid becoming vain because we have been placed over God's creation. A steward is only a caretaker. Although man should work to make his world a better place, he must remember that it is not really *his* world. The world belongs to God; man is only caring for it for a time.

Sometimes Christians tend to turn their backs on the world and try to avoid the responsibilities that are given to them as stewards, in these words of Genesis. At other times, they tend to work in and for the world and ignore the fact that they are dependent upon God, their Creator. Genesis tells us that we must move out into the world but at the same time keep our eyes on God, the Creator.

Man and woman. The creation account also tells us that man is not made to be alone. God made man and woman to be together, recognizing their need for companionship. Just as the Bible teaches that the world is good, it also teaches that the sex relationship is good. God made man and woman for each other, and sex is an important part of God's purpose for man.

All too often Christians think that the Bible condemns sex as evil. This is simply not true. The Bible sees sex realistically as both important and good. It warns against the evil of misusing sex, just as it urges us not to misuse any of God's gifts. But in our discussions about sex, we should remember that God has made us to need companions and to be companions. It is only our selfish abuse of this need that causes trouble.

To summarize, the creation account tells us that God did not just make us and leave us. It reveals that he continues to be near us and to be compassionate and sensitive to our needs in a good world that he made for us to live in.

B. The Call of Abraham

Abraham is one of the most important figures in the whole Bible. In his story (Gen. 12–25) we see God meeting a man in history, and we learn a great deal about both God and man. In chapter 12, we are told that Abraham lived in the land of his father until God said to him:

> Go from your country and your kindred and your
> father's house to the land that I will show you. And
> I will make of you a great nation, and I will bless you,
> and make your name great, so that you will be a
> blessing.

> Genesis 12:1-2

God called Abraham to leave his homeland and follow wherever God led. He made a *covenant,* or promise-agreement, with Abraham, pledging to give him a land in which his descendants would become a great nation. In this "call of Abraham" we see several significant things about the covenant relationship between God and man.

First, Abraham's story shows that God has not abandoned man. He actually enters human history to bless his followers. Second, the account shows that God requires first place in our loyalty. Abraham had to step out in faith and trust, putting God above his home, his family, and his friends. God also asks that we trust him above all other influences in our lives.

Third, we see that God does not necessarily call men because they are better than others. As a matter of fact, Abraham had fears and doubts and weaknesses like all men. God calls men to be righteous, honest, and obedient to him. But fortunately he does not wait until we are perfect before extending his promises.

Finally, Abraham's life teaches us something very important about the future. Abraham was led onward into a future he could not see. Yet he followed, because he trusted God. He was a man who lived by hope. The life of faith is one in which we trust God to guide, protect, and fulfill his promises. As the writer of Hebrews concludes:

> By faith Abraham obeyed when he was called to go out to a place which he was to receive as an inheritance; and he went out, not knowing where he was to go. By faith he sojourned in the land of promise, as in a foreign land, living in tents with Isaac and Jacob,

heirs with him of the same promise. For he looked forward to the city which has foundations, whose builder and maker is God.

Hebrews 11:8-10

C. The Exodus

The story of the exodus is one of the central stories in the whole Bible. The Israelites, descendants of Abraham and people of the covenant which God had made with him, became slaves in the land of Egypt. The exodus tells us that God once again acted in history. The second book of the Bible is called "Exodus," meaning "going out," because it tells the story of God delivering his covenant people from slavery in Egypt.

God called another man, Moses, to come to the aid of his people, the Israelites. After much difficulty, the Egyptian pharaoh, or king, allowed the Israelites to leave Egypt. But at the last moment he changed his mind and came after them with a vast army of chariots.

The frightened people were saved by a miraculous act of God. The waters of the Red Sea parted and the Israelites passed through on dry land! They found themselves in the desert wilderness of the Sinai peninsula (which you can find on Map D). But God was with them and led them in the form of a cloud by day and a pillar of fire by night (Exod. 13:21).

The account of the exodus clearly shows us the *faithfulness* of God and the *unfaithfulness* of his people. God reminded Moses:

> I have seen the affliction of my people who are in Egypt, and have heard their cry. . . . I know their sufferings, and I have come down to deliver them out of the hand of the Egyptians.

Exodus 3:7-8

God again is known as the deliverer and the God who acts in human affairs. And just as he called Abraham to leave his home, friends, and all the things that kept him from depending upon him, God led the Israelites into the wilderness where there was little water and less food. Only in this desperate situation were they able to see that their hope could only be in the God who delivers.

The exodus story tells us that God fed the people quail and a special food called manna. But God was concerned that the people no⁺ turn from him after getting their stomachs full. They were told to take only enough food to nourish them for a single day. They had to depend upon God for the bread of life.

Here again, as was the case with Abraham, we see that the Bible does not try to make superhuman heroes out of God's people. Even Moses' success in leading the people was not due to his own ability. When God called him to help in the great task of deliverance, Moses said, "Who am I that I should go to Pharaoh?" (Exod. 3:11). "They will not believe me or listen to my voice" (4:1). "Oh, my Lord, I am not eloquent . . . but I am slow of speech and of tongue" (4:10). But Moses could say, with the writer of Psalm 28:

The Lord is my strength and my shield;
in him my heart trusts.

Psalm 28:7

In sharp contrast to the faithfulness of God, the exodus account also tells us of the unfaithfulness of God's people. After all God had done for them, the people began to murmur against Moses and God (Exod. 15:22-25). Still, God did not abandon or disown them for their weakness. His strength was greater than their weakness.

The exodus is also connected with another important event in the history of God's great acts: the giving of the Law

(including the Ten Commandments). It is important to notice that God gave the Law to his people only after he had delivered them. First he showed his love for them by delivering them, and then he gave them the Law as a means of protecting them.

The Law was given in love because of the weakness of the people, not because God was trying to burden or condemn them. So, even when one kept the Law there was nothing for him to boast about; his strength still rested not in himself, but in God.

D. Kingdom and Exile

After wandering for forty years in the wilderness, Israel was led into the land that God had promised to Abraham long ago. As his people settled in the land, God led them in conquering those who opposed them. Whenever a crisis arose, God would call a "judge"—a special leader such as Gideon or Samson or the woman judge, Deborah.

Again and again Israel was unfaithful to God. The people became impressed by their neighbors and tried to copy their ways. Probably the biggest insult to God was their demand to have a king like the surrounding nations. God spoke to his people through Samuel:

> I brought up Israel out of Egypt, and I delivered you from the hand of the Egyptians and from the hand of all the kingdoms that were oppressing you. But you have this day rejected your God, who saves you from all your calamities and your distresses; and you have said, "No! but set a king over us."
>
> 1 Samuel 10:18-19

So it was under these circumstances that Israel, the people chosen by God, came to have a king. God remained faithful and yielded to the weakness of the people, giving them the man Saul as a king.

There were several great kings after Saul, but probably the most highly respected were David and his son, Solomon. Under the reign of King Solomon, the little country grew larger and its fame reached many lands. It is extremely important to notice what the success of the David-Solomon kingdom did to the faith of the people.

First, there was a real temptation to think that the kingdom, now famous, was the final goal of God. Many felt that it was for this purpose that God had called Abraham hundreds of years earlier.

Second, there was also a temptation for the people to place their faith in the king and the nation rather than in God. They had difficulty learning not to place more confidence in their nation and their money than they had in God.

After Solomon, Israel fell into worse and worse times. The

country became divided into two separate kingdoms, the Northern Kingdom (Israel) and the Southern Kingdom (Judah).

The story of the two kingdoms is a
grim story of unfaithfulness. The
Northern Kingdom came under the
influence of false gods, especially
Baal. The people forgot the God of
creation, Abraham, and the exodus. Finally, in 721 B.C.,
after the people had sunk so low as to sacrifice their own children to the pagan god Moloch, God allowed them to be conquered and carried off into captivity by the nation of Assyria
(2 Kings 17).

After the destruction of the Northern Kingdom, only Judah
remained. Judah, however, was also filled with the wickedness that had infested Israel. Her kings turned from God
repeatedly. In reading the story of Judah's kings, one reads
again and again, "And the king did what was evil in the sight of
the Lord. . . ." So the story goes until we finally read:

> And the Lord said, "I will remove Judah also out of
> my sight, as I have removed Israel, and I will cast off
> this city which I have chosen, Jerusalem, and the
> house of which I said, My name shall be there."
>
> 2 Kings 23:27

However, the unfaithfulness of God's people did not go
completely unnoticed in the nation. The history of the two
kingdoms is also the history of Israel's great prophets.

We tend to think of the prophets only as men who could see
into the future. They also spoke to God's people a message
that warned against false religion and pride. They continually
reminded the people of their unfaithfulness. *Amos* was typical

of these prophets when he spoke the following words of God:

> I hate, I despise your feasts,
>   and I take no delight in your solemn assemblies.
> Even though you offer me your burnt offerings and
>   cereal offerings,
>   I will not accept them,
> and the peace offerings of your fatted beasts
>   I will not look upon.
> Take away from me the noise of your songs;
>   to the melody of your harps I will not listen.
> But let justice roll down like waters,
>   and righteousness like an everflowing stream.
>
> Amos 5:21-24

What a condemnation! God's people had become so corrupt that even their worship was meaningless in God's sight. Through the prophet, God said that the people had missed the whole point. He wanted them to understand that justice and doing right are what the law is intended to bring about, and that they are more important than outward signs of religion.

Because of their unfaithfulness, God also allowed the Southern Kingdom to be conquered by a foreign nation. Judah fell to the Babylonians in 586 B.C. They had come to trust in themselves and in the belief that God would always protect them no matter how unfaithful they were.

But even before the final collapse of the kingdom, the prophet Jeremiah looked forward in hope to a distant event:

> Behold the days are coming, says the Lord, when I
> will make a new covenant with the house of Israel
> and the house of Judah, not like the covenant which I
> made with their fathers when I took them by the hand
> to bring them out of the land of Egypt, my covenant
> which they broke. . . . I will put my law within them,

and I will write it upon their hearts; and I will be their God and they shall be my people. . . . I will forgive their iniquity and I will remember their sin no more.

Jeremiah 31:31-34

God's people could look forward to a time when God would renew the covenant he had kept with them from the time he had called Abraham. Knowing the faithfulness of God, the people trusted that he would act again. A remnant was allowed to return to Jerusalem; but they knew neither when nor how God's next acts would appear in the story of their nation.

For over two hundred years God's people waited for the *Messiah*—the one anointed, or chosen, by God to deliver them from their enemies. It is in this setting of anxious waiting and hoping that God finally acted again. But this is the story of the New Testament.

5

THE STORY OF THE NEW TESTAMENT

PART ONE: THE STORY OF JESUS

A. The Coming of Jesus

The New Testament is a story about real people and real places. It tells of God's most exciting and important act. It is the story of Jesus, who was God's anointed, the Messiah. To understand the New Testament better, it is necessary to know something of the social and political conditions of that time.

God's people, the Jews, were at this time still ruled by a foreign nation. They had come under the great Roman Empire with its capital in Rome. Although they were allowed religious freedom, the Jews were not free to control all their affairs. Roman soldiers and Roman rulers carried out orders received from Rome.

The Jews looked back in history to those days when they were ruled by their own kings—the great kings like David and Solomon. Thinking about the past and living in constant contact with foreign soldiers of occupation, the Jews now anxiously awaited the overthrow of the Romans. They began to expect a Messiah who would forcibly drive out the Romans and set up another kingdom like the kingdom of David.

It was in this setting that God chose to act. He acted in Jesus of Nazareth, who is the fullest revelation of what God is like. Jesus said that anyone "who sees me sees him who sent me" (John 12:45). So in Jesus, more clearly than ever before or after, the God-Who-Delivers makes himself known to men.

Through Jesus, God established a new covenant with men, the covenant to which men had looked forward and for which they had hoped from the times of the prophets. Like the old covenant, the new one shows God's concern and compassion for men. It also shows God's willingness to act for man's good.

Though there are many differences between the old and new covenants, one of the main differences has to do with who Jesus was. The writer of Hebrews put it this way:

> In many and various ways God spoke of old to our fathers by the prophets; but in these last days he has spoken to us by a Son, whom he appointed the heir of all things, through whom also he created the world. He reflects the glory of God and bears the very stamp of his nature, upholding the universe by his word of power. When he had made purification for sins, he sat down at the right hand of the Majesty on high, having become as much superior to angels as the name he has obtained is more excellent than theirs.
>
> Hebrews 1:1-4

We cannot miss the fact that Jesus is God's Son! The word "son" does not mean quite the same here as it does when we say that we are the sons of our fathers. It means that Jesus had a very special relationship with God—greater than those of any of the great leaders and prophets of the Old Testament.

But, more important, it means that God himself was in Christ.

The most startling fact about Jesus dawns on us when the Bible calls him "the Word of God." The term *logos,* which is Greek for "word" or "speech," is used to describe God's power in speaking the world into existence: "And God *said,* Let there be light." But when the gospel of John speaks of Jesus, it describes him also as *the Word:*

A WORD FOR THE WISE

Logos

(LOG-os), Greek for "speech, word, or reason," appears in many English words:

- theo*logy* = theos (God) + logos, and means reasoning about, or the study of, God.
- bio*logy* = bios (life) + logos, or the study of living things.
- *logi*cal = speaking in a way that makes sense.

To think of Jesus as the *logos,* or "reason" of God, is to say that his way makes the world make sense!

> In the beginning was the Word, and the Word was with God, and the Word was God. He was in the beginning with God; all things were made through him, and without him was not anything made that was made. . . . And the Word became flesh and dwelt among us, full of grace and truth. . . .
>
> John 1:1-3, 14

Imagine that! In some way, Jesus was present as the creative power of God when the world was made. And yet, his birth in Bethlehem means that he was willing to live in the world, where we live. He was the Word-made-flesh.

But this, God's greatest act, was not in the form of a show of power—at least not right away. It was in the form of a helpless baby, born to a lowly Jewish couple named Joseph and Mary.

B. The Life of Jesus

The New Testament begins with the coming of a new baby

to the little town of Bethlehem, a story familiar to all of us. The earth-shaking message of the New Testament, however, is that the great God of the creation was active in history again, this time in a baby. The importance of this event is made clear in the announcement of the angel to Mary:

> . . . you shall call his name Jesus.
> He will be great, and will be called
>   the Son of the Most High;
> and the Lord God will give to him the throne of his
>   father David,
> and he will reign over the house of Jacob for ever;
> and of his kingdom there will be no end.
>
> Luke 1:31-33

Yet, as we shall see, the way in which Jesus was to be heir to the throne of David created a problem. Because the people expected the Messiah to be a king like David, the religious leaders and most of the people did not accept Jesus. The way God confronted his people caught many of them off guard. There were three main reasons.

First, Jesus kept company with sinners. Religious people probably expected God to be more favorable to them. When the Messiah came, they thought he would associate with those who separated themselves from sinners and from matters of everyday life. But Jesus did not do this. Once he was eating with a group of sinners when some of the Pharisees, very religious Jewish people, saw him. In those days and in that land, eating with someone was a sign of closeness. So the Pharisees asked him, "Why do you eat and drink with tax collectors and sinners?" (Luke 5:30).

We must remember that probably the greatest hope of their lives was that they might live to see the Messiah come in power and glory and deliver their people. And so when they rushed to see Jesus, hoping that this teacher might turn out to be the Messiah, they could hardly help but be bitterly disappointed. Here he sat at a table with a few dusty, ignorant peasants. And, still worse, sitting with them was a tax collector—one of  those despised fellows who had agreed to collect taxes for the hated Romans!

But Jesus knew that they had failed to understand something very important. He told them, "Those who are well have no need of a physician, but those who are sick; I have not come to call the righteous, but sinners to repentance" (Luke 5:31-32).

A second reason that Jesus was not what the Jewish people expected was that he came to serve. Not only was he interested in sinners; he also came to serve them. This was hard even for his followers to understand.

Just before his death, Jesus surprised and shocked his disciples while they were eating together. On his knees with a basin of water, Jesus began to wash their feet! Could this be the Messiah, the one who would deliver God's people? Many began to think it could not be. Even Jesus' disciples were unsure, because no one expected the Messiah to be a servant. But the gospels quote Jesus as saying that he came not to be served, but to serve (Matt. 20:28; Mark 10:45).

The third reason that the Jewish people were surprised at Jesus was that he came to suffer. Jesus saw himself as the servant of God of whom the prophet Isaiah had spoken:

> He had no form or comeliness that we should look
>   at him,
>   and no beauty that we should desire him.

> He was despised and rejected by men;
>   a man of sorrows, and acquainted with grief. . . .
> He was oppressed, and he was afflicted,
>   yet he opened not his mouth;
> like a lamb that is led to the slaughter,
>   and like a sheep that before his shearers is dumb,
>   so he opened not his mouth.
>
> Isaiah 53:2-3, 7

On one occasion, Peter called Jesus the Christ—or Messiah—in answer to Jesus' question, "Who do you think I am?" After Peter made this answer, Jesus began to tell his followers that he would suffer:

> And he began to teach them that the Son of man [a name Jesus used for himself] must suffer many things, and be rejected by the elders and the chief priests and scribes, and be killed.
>
> Mark 8:31

Imagine the shock of finding that the Messiah was not the great warrior that was expected! And even harder to believe was that he would actually suffer—so much that he must die.

C. The Cross

All four gospels tell of the death of Jesus. The story of the cross is the story of Jesus being left alone by his followers. Even Peter, one of the disciples closest to him, ran away when Jesus was taken by the soldiers and would not admit that he even knew him. Jesus was taken before both the Jewish and Roman authorities, mocked, and tortured. Then he walked the lonely road to the hill Golgotha (which means "the skull"), painfully carrying the heavy cross on which he was to die. Just as in the Old Testament, here is God's act of faithfulness amidst the unfaithfulness of man.

Even when he was on the cross and in the greatest of pain, Jesus still had thoughts of others. He thought of a dying robber on a nearby cross and said, "Today you will be with me in Paradise" (Luke 23:43). He thought of his mother, Mary, and asked one of his followers to take care of her (John 19:25-27). He even thought of the

Roman soldiers and the crowd who had helped to put him here: "Father, forgive them; for they know not what they do" (Luke 23:34).

The cross, which stands for the suffering and death of Jesus (see 1 Cor. 1:17-18), tells of both man and God. What the cross says about man is painful to hear. The cross tells us that ignorant men, proud men, thrill seekers, selfish men, all had a hand in the death of God's Son.

But what the cross says about God is what gives us our hope and gives meaning to Jesus' suffering. The apostle Paul said:

> While we were still weak, at the right time Christ died for the ungodly. Why, one will hardly die for a righteous man—though perhaps for a good man one will dare to die. But God shows his love for us in that while we were yet sinners Christ died for us.
>
> Romans 5:6-8

Christ did not die for us because we were so good. The Bible says that God gave his Son for sinners—for the lowest of men—because of his love (John 3:16).

D. The Resurrection

The story of the cross tells of a frightened, disappointed little group of men and women who had followed Jesus. All their hopes and expectations were gone when their leader was killed. Had they wasted three years following the great teacher? They had learned a lot from him but now he was dead. He had been executed, as if he were a criminal, on a cross.

If the story of the New Testament ended at this point, we would be faced with a problem. How is this good news? How does this story help us? Of course, it does show something of God's love; yet, if it ended here, the story would come to a sad end.

But the New Testament tells us that this is not the end of the story. All the gospels shout that God raised Jesus from the grave! Once again God is shown to be the God-Who-Delivers. God delivered Jesus from the grave, and he appeared to his followers only three days after his burial. The disciples were taken by surprise, for they were not expecting Jesus to be raised. Some couldn't even believe it when they saw Jesus. Thomas said that unless he could see and touch the nailprints in Jesus' hands and touch the wound in his side, he wouldn't believe (John 20:25).

Jesus allowed Thomas to touch his wounds and prove for himself that his teacher was really alive. But then he asked

Thomas and his other followers to trust and have faith in God and in him as the Christ (or Messiah) of God. The last time he was with them Jesus gave his followers what has been called the "Great Commission."

> All authority in heaven and on earth has been given to me. Go therefore and make disciples of all nations, baptizing them in the name of the Father and of the Son and of the Holy Spirit, teaching them to observe all that I have commanded you; and lo, I am with you always, to the close of the age.
>
> Matthew 28:18-20

The resurrection of Jesus Christ tells us that God is able to deliver life from death—and this is one of the greatest fears and uncertainties that men face. The resurrection means that we can have faith and trust in God to be with us and to deliver us from death.

E. Lord and Christ

The resurrection also tells us something about Jesus. It says that all authority has been given to him. Or, as Peter says in a famous sermon, "Let all the house of Israel therefore know assuredly that God has made both Lord and Christ, this Jesus whom you crucified" (Acts 2:36). "Lord and Christ" may not mean much to us today. "Christ," for example, is not a proper name. Sometimes we say "Jesus Christ" like we would say "Bill Jones" or "Mary Smith." The term "Christ," however, comes from the Greek word *Christos* from which we get our word "christen" as in the christening of a ship. The Hebrew word "Messiah" means "anointed," and this is what Peter means when he says that Jesus is the Christ. He is the Messiah—the chosen one of God who will deliver God's people. Peter is saying, "God raised him. He is the one!" And when Peter says that Jesus is "Lord," he uses the Greek word *Kyrios,* which means one who rules with total authority. He means that Jesus has such power and authority that to honor God one must know Jesus as Lord. To hear God one must hear Jesus; to know God one must know Jesus. Paul states:

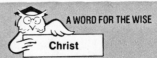

A WORD FOR THE WISE

Christ

This word should give the followers of Jesus a special purpose in life. The Greek word *christos* meant "anointed." Later, "christening" came to refer to the anointing that gives one a special name—as at the christening of a ship commissioned for a special voyage.

When the disciples were given the new name "Christian" (Acts 11:26), one might say they were commissioned to make any voyage necessary to tell others of Christ, the Messiah.

God has highly exalted him and bestowed on him the name which is above every name, that at the name of Jesus every knee should bow, in heaven and on earth and under the earth, and every tongue confess that Jesus Christ is Lord, to the glory of God the Father.

Philippians 2:9-10

6

THE STORY OF THE NEW TESTAMENT

PART TWO: THE STORY OF THE EARLY CHURCH

God's new covenant with men is based on the life, death, and resurrection of Jesus. Through Jesus, man and God enter into a new relationship. In Jesus, God delivers men from sin, from fear, and from their own mean and selfish lives. They are called to give themselves entirely to him and to try to do his will. They are called to tell the good news to other men.

The early church was first made up of those who had personally traveled with Jesus and seen him after the resurrection. These men, called "apostles" (meaning "ones sent"), were the first Christian preachers. Through them, others came to accept Jesus as the Christ and Lord. With the guidance and help of the Holy Spirit, the early church grew and spread. This part of the story of the New Testament is found in the book of Acts, or Acts of the Apostles.

A. The Church as a New Community

Because of Jesus Christ, the early Christians knew that they shared in a new relationship with God. They knew how greatly God loved them and that it was his desire for men to love and trust him. They had entered into a new covenant with him, a covenant even greater than the one which their fathers had broken. This new relationship was based on Jesus and what he had shown about God.

The new covenant had still another side to it. Because the new Christians all worshiped Jesus as Lord, and God as the Father of all, they also had a new relationship with one another. Together they formed a new community. They shared a loyalty to one Lord, a belief that God acts in history, their commitment to the teachings of Jesus, and their future hope.

The new community formed by the followers of Jesus is called by several names in the New Testament. One of the earliest was "the Way" (Acts 9:2; 19:9; 22:4). Paul the apostle called it a "holy temple" and "dwelling place of God" (Eph. 2:21-22), and the "body of Christ" (1 Cor. 12:27). He compared the church with a bride who is subject to her husband (Eph. 5:21-24). All of these are ways of describing the community of Christians we usually call the church.

The early church showed in many ways what it means to be a body of followers of Jesus. To begin with, these Christians had come into the church through their repentance from their sins, confession of Christ as Lord, and baptism into him. Now they tried to live so that their lives reflected the love of Jesus Christ for all men. This does not mean that they always lived just as they should or as God would want them to. The book of

Acts and the letters of the New Testament tell us that they failed in many ways. They were only ordinary men and women; and, as in the Old Testament, God had called these people not because they already were righteous but in order to make them righteous (1 Pet. 2:9-10).

Immediately after Peter preached the first sermon on the day of Pentecost following Jesus' resurrection, about three thousand people repented of their sins and were baptized into Christ, forming his church (Acts 2:41). By taking a look at these people, we can get an idea of what the earliest church was like in its day-to-day life. Here is how Luke described them:

> And they devoted themselves to the apostles' teaching and fellowship, to the breaking of bread and the prayers. And fear came upon every soul; and many wonders and signs were done through the apostles. And all who believed were together and had all things in common; and they sold their possessions and goods and distributed them to all, as any had need. And day by day, attending the temple together and breaking bread in their homes, they partook of food with glad and generous hearts, praising God and having favor with all the people. And the Lord added to their number day by day those who were being saved.

> Acts 2:42-47

We learn from this description several things about the new Christians. They were eager to study and learn more about Jesus and his teachings. They were anxious to spend as much time as possible in worship and fellowship. They were generous in helping any who had need, just as Jesus had been. And they continually spread the good news of Jesus to others.

B. The Universal Church

One important thing that made the new covenant different from the old is the fact that it was open to all people and not intended for just one chosen nation. We can speak of the church, then, as a "universal" church, meaning that all people of any race, nation, and background are welcome into it.

The very earliest church, however, was made up almost entirely of Jewish people. They were the nation who was expecting a Messiah; and though most of them rejected Jesus as not being the type of Messiah they looked for, still the gospel was preached to them first. In fact, the early church borrowed many of its forms of worship from the synagogue worship. The synagogues were small religious centers, built wherever Jews lived, to which they would go for worship and study of scripture. Some of the earliest Christian sermons were preached to Jewish audiences in synagogues (for example, see Acts 13:15-43).

But Jesus had told his followers the last time he was with them to "make disciples of all nations" (Matt. 28:19), and this included taking the good news to *Gentiles,* or non-Jews. Jews and Gentiles had looked at each other as enemies, but now they were to become brothers in Jesus Christ.

The first New Testament story of the conversion of a Gentile to Christianity is the story of Cornelius (Acts 10:1–11:18). The fact that Luke gave so much space and time to this event in his writing shows us that it was a matter of great importance to the early church. At this time, some of the Jews who accepted Jesus Christ and became members of the early church still saw the new way as another covenant between God and the Jewish nation. But after this event, they had to realize that Jesus had come to save all people of all nations.

Cornelius was a Roman centurion, a soldier of important rank. Though he was not a member of the Jewish nation, he and his family worshiped God, prayed constantly, and gave to the poor. One day he had a vision in which God told him to send for a man named Peter. Cornelius did so immediately.

The next day, while Cornelius' servants were traveling to find Peter, Peter himself was on a rooftop in prayer. Then he, too, had a vision. He saw a great sheet let down from the sky, filled with animals and birds of all kinds. He heard God's voice say to him, "Rise, Peter; kill and eat." But Peter would not, for these animals were forbidden food in the Jewish laws. Then God's voice came again to Peter: "What God has cleansed, you must not call common." The same thing happened again two more times, and Peter was unable to understand what it meant.

Meanwhile, the messenger from Cornelius arrived at the house where Peter was staying while he was still thinking about the vision. They called for him from the gate. The Spirit told Peter that he was to go with them. He immediately came down from his rooftop and went with them to Cornelius' house. Cornelius, expecting him, had called a number of his friends together. When he met them, Peter said:

"You yourselves know how unlawful it is for a Jew to associate with or to visit any one of another nation; but God has shown me that I should not call any man common or unclean."

Acts 10:28

Peter preached the gospel to this gathering of Gentiles, and those who heard him were baptized into Jesus Christ.

This event caused quite a stir among the Jewish Christians. Some who heard that Peter had visited with Gentiles and eaten with them were very disturbed, and they called Peter before them to explain his conduct. He told them the story of his vision, and he told them what he now knew that it meant. He told how the Spirit had instructed him to go with the messengers and how he had found the eager group waiting for him at Cornelius' house. And then Peter asked them:

"Who was I that I could withstand God?" When they heard this they were silenced. And they glorified God, saying, "Then to the Gentiles also God has granted repentance unto life."

Acts 11:17-18

From that time on, the mission of the church grew broader. Paul, the apostle who came to be known as "the apostle to the Gentiles," was talking about the unity of all people in the church of Jesus Christ when he said that "There is neither Jew nor Greek, there is neither slave nor free, there is neither male nor female; for you are all one in Christ Jesus" (Gal. 3:28). Jesus had broken down the "wall" that divided them, as nothing else had been able to do (Eph. 2:14; Col. 3:11).

C. The Missionary Church

Now the church was eager to spread the good news of Jesus

to all lands and all people, since they understood that God intended the gospel for all. The church in Antioch was the first to decide that one of the ways it would work to bring the gospel to the world was by sending out men to travel from country to country and preach.

Paul and Barnabas were chosen to make this first missionary journey. You can trace their travels on the map of these journeys (See map F). First they sailed to the island of Cyprus, in the Mediterranean Sea, and then north to the mainland of Asia Minor. There they visited several cities in the province of Galatia. They often went to the Jewish synagogues on the regular days of meeting and spoke to those who met there. After visiting a number of places, Paul and Barnabas turned around and went back through the cities they had already visited. They encouraged the new Christians, taught them more about Jesus, organized them into churches, and helped them choose leaders among themselves.

The missionaries did many good works and found many people ready to listen to their words, but they also had many problems. In one city, some angered people tried to kill Paul by throwing stones at him, and he very nearly died there. But when the group returned to Antioch, they were able to report that God had "opened a door of faith to the Gentiles" (Acts 14:27).

Later Paul and Barnabas separated to make new journeys (See map F), Paul taking Silas with him and Barnabas taking John Mark. Paul and Silas went back to all the new churches that had been begun in Galatia on the first trip. Timothy joined them at Lystra. They traveled in Asia Minor and then in

Macedonia, across the Aegean Sea. As Paul preached in the cities there, he again went first to the synagogues. But once again, he found Gentiles more ready to listen than Jews.

The longest stop on this second trip was in Corinth, where Paul stayed for about a year and a half. He worked as a tentmaker while continuing to preach to all who would listen. Then he went back across the Aegean to visit Ephesus, across the Mediterranean to Jerusalem, and back north to Antioch.

The third time he left Antioch (See Map G), Paul went back to a great many of the young churches he had helped to start. When he came to Ephesus, there was so much good work he could do that he stayed for nearly three years. While he was there, he began making a collection for the church in Jerusalem, where the church was made up mostly of Jewish people, many of them poor. By the time he reached Jerusalem, he had a large collection from the mostly Gentile churches he had visited. But in Jerusalem Paul ran into trouble with the Jewish authorities. He was arrested and imprisoned. After some time, he was transferred to Rome (See Map G), where his case was to go before Roman authorities.

After a journey that included a terrible storm and a shipwreck, Paul arrived in Rome. When the book of Acts ends, Paul is still imprisoned in Rome, but the Romans were allowing him to stay in a house, with only one soldier guarding him. He used his time to write many of the letters which are included in our New Testament. It appears that Paul was released after about two years so that he was able to do some more traveling (1 Tim.

1:3; 3:14) before he was imprisoned again (2 Tim. 1:16-17; 2:9; 4:16-18) and finally put to death in Rome.

Paul was one of the first great missionaries of the early church, but by the time of his death, a great many Christians were teaching and preaching in many lands. All the Christians in the young church, no matter where they were living or what their daily tasks were, believed that they too, could spread the gospel by the way that they lived. They could show the love of God in Christ by obeying his commands and being kind and loving to other people. This living teaching, which is still important in the life of every Christian, worked with the teaching of the missionaries to cause the good news of Jesus to reach many people.

D. The Writings of the Church

A large part of our New Testament is made up of letters written to churches or to individual Christians, as we discussed in chapter 3. Only a few of the followers of Jesus Christ in the early church had actually seen or heard him, and since there was not a book of writings about him available at that early time, letters were used for teaching new Christians. They were also used to spread news among the churches, such as the information that Paul was taking up a collection for the Jerusalem church (1 Cor. 16:1-4). They nearly always contained some personal greetings, too.

Some of these letters were sent by messengers from church to church, so that many groups of Christians could learn from the writers. In fact, it is thought that the letter to the Ephesians was actually intended as a "circular" letter to be sent around to many congregations.

After a long while, the leaders of the church realized that the apostles and those who had been with Jesus during his lifetime were dying. They began to collect their writings so that the church could have a lasting record of them. You can read about how this collection became our New Testament in chapter 7.

We know that many problems occurred in the early church, because the letters of Paul and others tell us about them. But we also know that the Spirit was with these early Christians, guiding and aiding them in their efforts to live as Jesus lived and taught, and to tell the good news about him to others. And we have the promise that this same Spirit will be with us today as we continue the work of the church.

7

THE AUTHORITY AND INSPIRATION OF THE BIBLE

A. How We Learn

Your way of life is affected by what you know. For example, if you know that a bus trip downtown from your home costs thirty cents, you will make certain that you have the fare before getting on the bus. If you know that you don't have the fare, you will either walk or postpone your trip.

We all try to make our plans for the future on the basis of what we know. And we come to know things in several ways. First, we may find out for ourselves, through experience. A young boy, for instance, may not know that tying a knot in the garden hose will make it leak until after he has tried it (and maybe even been punished). He learns from experience how the hose is affected. We learn things by experience every day as we become acquainted with new surroundings and new friends.

Another way we learn or come to know things is through someone else. That is, we may not personally experience something firsthand but may experience it through someone else.

Your dad might tell you that pouring hot lead into a wet container will cause a dangerous explosion. You may avoid an accident if you learn from him this way—perhaps one that your dad experienced firsthand. If we could not learn through the experience of others, each of us would have to start at the very beginning. The exploration of outer space is a good example of the way we learn from the experience of others.  Each space flight gains knowledge that the next flight is able to use. Knowledge that comes through others can be learned faster and in greater amounts. So, in a sense, knowledge that is not firsthand—or from one's personal experience—is no less valuable than knowledge from our own experience.

There is still another way in which we learn things. We come to know things through the use of our minds in what we call reasoning. You may know that Betty is five years older than Mike. You do not know Mike's age but you know that Betty is eleven. You may use the knowledge that you have and reason your way to knowing Mike's age.

We do this every day. You step into the street and notice that the pavement is wet. You may think that either it has just rained or a street cleaner has recently passed. From the fact that the grass is also wet and that heavy clouds are in the sky, you may decide that it has definitely rained. This knowledge, however, is based on reason and has not been experienced. That is, you did not actually see and feel the rain.

What we know has a definite effect on the way we live. And we come to know things by experience, by reason, or by depending upon someone else to tell us of their experience.

B. Knowledge through God's Word

We can come to know God, too. But our highest knowledge of him does not come through reason or experience. The Bible tells us how God is known through *revelation*. This means that God *reveals* himself in ways that human wisdom alone cannot discover. It is knowledge that can come only from God.

God has done this in the history of Israel. You recall how in the Old Testament God called Abraham, led his people out of the Egyptian captivity in the exodus, and again and again acted in their history. The Bible tells us that God spoke to special men of his choosing and gave them "revelations"—messages to take to his people.

But the fullest revelation of God was in Jesus of Nazareth. The writer of Hebrews in the New Testament writes:

> In many and various ways God spoke of old to our fathers by the prophets; but in these last days he has spoken to us by a Son, whom he appointed the heir of all things, through whom also he created the world. He [Jesus] reflects the glory of God and bears the very stamp of his nature, upholding the universe by his word of power.

Hebrews 1:1-3

This is the New Testament faith, and this is really what Christianity is all about. Because Jesus Christ reveals God to us in a special way, he is even called "the Word of God" (read John 1:1, 18). In Jesus, God reveals *himself,* not just something about himself (read John 12:45).

But how do we see and understand Jesus? We obviously cannot walk along the shore of the Sea of Galilee with him . . . or can we? As a matter of fact, we can—in a sense. We can see and come to know Jesus, the Word, through the pages of the New Testament. Thus, the Bible itself comes to be "the word of God." The New Testament reports to us the life, death, and resurrection of Jesus, written by actual witnesses of God's actions in Jesus. As one of the New Testament writers put it:

> That which . . . we have heard, which we have seen with our eyes, which we have looked upon and touched with our hands, concerning the word of life [Jesus]—the life was made manifest, and we saw it, and testify to it, and proclaim to you the eternal life which was with the Father and was made manifest to us—that which we have seen and heard we proclaim to you.
>
> 1 John 1:1-3

C. The Authority of Scripture

We might ask whether the New Testament witnesses can be depended on to be true. Witnesses in courtroom trials are not always reliable. Some witnesses lie for money and others are honest but mistaken. Perhaps they don't see or remember well or for some other reason are not too dependable.

Some have raised the same questions about the Bible and its authors. To be fair we should look at their questions. We must use our minds as we consider God's revelation in the Bible.

Someone years ago suggested that Jesus never even lived —that there was no such person. This is a curious theory, but it is not very sensible. How could such a person as Jesus have been dreamed up? And even more important, does it make any sense to think that the followers of Jesus would have made up such a story and then given their lives for a lie?

It seems far more reasonable to believe that Jesus lived and impressed men as someone special, than to think that he never even lived! A study of Jesus' followers shows that they were certainly not simple-minded or dishonest. On the contrary, they were very honest and intelligent. They told in a straightforward and unashamed way of their own slow and painful acceptance of Jesus as the Christ. Some of us might be tempted to leave out part of the story, but these men stuck to the truth—even when it meant telling of their own betrayal of their friend Jesus. They were intelligent. For example, Luke (who wrote Luke and Acts) was a doctor and probably spoke both Hebrew and Greek. It doesn't make sense to think that these men intentionally lied.

The very foundation of the church is the witness of the apostles to what God did in Jesus. The writers of the Old and New Testaments are the source of our knowledge of what God has done, is doing, and will do in the future.

The role of the apostles as eyewitness to Jesus of Nazareth is something that can never happen again. There is no way that anyone else can be an apostle. Just as we can have no more witnesses to the assassination of President Lincoln, there can be no more "going back" to Jesus. We must depend upon the witnesses that we have in the New Testament—and these witnesses are dependable.

D. The Inspiration of Scripture

But God has not left us depending merely on human witnesses. We are told God protected his witnesses and guided them in their reporting and understanding of this revelation in Christ. This brings us to the concept of inspiration.

When we speak about inspiration, we are talking about what Paul said about scripture in 2 Timothy 3:16. Scripture, he said, is "inspired by God." The word Paul uses means "God-breathed" or "filled with the breath of God." The Bible's claim for itself is very clear: God is the moving power in the writing of scripture.

As God spoke through the apostles and other Spirit-filled men of the early church, this inspiration was the fulfillment of the promise of Jesus that the Holy Spirit would be sent to guide the apostles. Jesus promised his disciples that "the Holy Spirit . . . will teach you all things, and bring to your remembrance all that I have said to you" (John 14:26).

How did God inspire the biblical writers? Read

A WORD FOR THE WISE

Inspiration

This word sounds something like "respiration," which refers to breathing. Sure enough, *inspiration* of scripture means that God "breathed" his message into his writers. The English word *inspire* comes from the Latin *inspirare*, to breathe into. Paul uses the Greek word *theopneustos* in 2 Tim. 3:16. You have already met the word *theos*, God. *Pneuma* is Greek for wind, breath, or soul. (A *pneumatic* drill runs on air.)

theos + pneustos = God-breathed

again Hebrews 1:1-2. First, we are told that God has inspired men in the past. Further, this was done in "many and various ways." Inspiration does not necessarily mean that God dictated his message word for word. Although this might have been true in some cases, God's Spirit did not make these men write something completely without the use of their own intelligence or reason.

Luke, the physician who wrote approximately one-fourth of the New Testament, tells us that he "followed all things closely for some times past" (Luke 1:3). In other words, Luke did research. We know from reading the four gospels that these inspired writers wrote about many of the same events, but their different ways of telling about them shows us something about their own personalities. The important point is not *how* the Bible is inspired but *that it is*. The Bible tells us that it is inspired. We know that in the Bible we have God's will for us. We may feel sure that God inspired the writers of the Bible in whatever way achieved his purpose.

The second point made by Hebrews 1:1-2 is just as important. In times past—in the Old Testament—God spoke to and through various men, but he speaks to us today through Jesus Christ. It is in Jesus that all of the books of the Bible find their meaning.

All of the writers of the New Testament tell us in some way that "God was in Christ reconciling the world to himself" (2 Cor. 5:19). The person who reads the Bible and overlooks this point is like a biology student who becomes more fascinated with his microscope than the slide he is supposed to be examining.

Another question that comes up when we discuss the Bible is, "Do we have all of the inspired writings of the early church?" The answer is no—in all honesty, we probably do not. Neither do we know all of the things that Jesus said and did.

> But there are many other things which Jesus did; were every one of them to be written, I suppose that the world itself could not contain the books that would be written.
>
> John 21:25

We know that the apostle Paul wrote at least one other letter to the Corinthian church (see 1 Cor. 5:9) and possibly more (see Col. 4:16). What we have in the New Testament is a selection, guided by the Holy Spirit, from the body of inspired writings that the early church possessed. We may be sure, however, that those other writings did not differ in substance from those which we now possess.

Sometimes we hear men today speak as if their own writings were inspired just as the Bible is. However, as we have mentioned, the Bible reveals Christ to us. God's revelation in Jesus was witnessed by the apostles and other closely associated men in the early church who were guided by God in their writings. No other revelation about God is necessary (Gal. 1:8).

E. What the Bible's Authority and Inspiration Mean to Us

Since the Bible is the inspired word of God, it should be our final authority in religion. There is, however, a popular view that religion is something so personal and private that one understanding is just as good as another. While it is true that religion—especially the Christian faith—is very personal, this does not mean that there can be no authority in Christianity. Sometimes this sort of view is held by people who do not want to sound critical of the views and beliefs of others. Sometimes it is held by those wanting to be "democratic" or "fair" to others.

Regardless of the reason and how well-intentioned the view, the idea that religious authority can be a matter of personal like and dislike is not Christianity. This really amounts to little other than the view that a person may make up his own religion by picking and choosing those things that he wishes Jesus had said and ignoring those he wishes Jesus had not said. In this way of understanding religious authority, a person's own selfish desires and personal views are his only authority.

Another view gives total authority in religion to special people (either a select group or an individual). This view says that ordinary men are not intelligent enough to understand

God's will and must have it interpreted for them. It leaves the impression that there are men today who are holier than others and stand closer to God so that they are able to make his will known to us. Some people believe that when a person wants to pray, he cannot do it on his own but must go to one of these special representatives of God. Thus religious authority is placed in some man or group of men.

A danger is that often people holding this view come to think they have no responsibility to think or worship for themselves. They let someone do their thinking and worshiping for them. They are always depending upon someone else to explain their faith to them. Though adults, they remain as children.

The Bible teaches that God has given man the written word as the final religious authority. Instead of obeying custom, some individual, or group of special people, Christians are given God's word, the Bible.

As a person reads the Bible, he comes into direct contact with inspired men who recorded God's will. It is through the study of the Bible that we come to know God. Only through the Bible do we see Jesus and learn what God is like—that he is the Creator, the one who delivers, and the one who loves us. In the Bible, we learn what God wants us to do, and who God wants us to be.

8

HOW TO STUDY THE BIBLE

A. The Importance of Bible Study

The Bible is the story of what God has done for us. It tells us about God and man; and because of its great wisdom in these matters, people of all ages should enjoy reading the Bible. Many men have recognized the Bible's importance and the value of studying it. Notice what some great men have said about the Bible:

The Bible is endorsed by the ages. Our civilization is built upon its words. In no other book is there such a collection of inspired wisdom, reality, and hope.

Dwight D. Eisenhower

The Bible is a book in comparison with which all others in my eyes are of minor importance and which in all my perplexities and distresses has never failed to give me light and strength.

Robert E. Lee

We account the Scriptures of God to be the most sublime philosophy. I find more sure marks of authenticity in the Bible than in any profane history whatever.

Sir Isaac Newton

B. Some Helps in Bible Study

Great men have recognized the quality and value of the Bible and man's continuing need for reading the "Book of Books." Here are some ways we can make our own Bible reading more helpful and enjoyable.

1. *You need to have your own Bible to study and read.* There is no need to spend a great deal of money on a Bible. The important thing is to get a translation that you can easily understand and one which has type that is large enough to be easy on your eyes. You should feel free to underline or write in your Bible just as you would do in any of your other personal study books.

2. *Set aside a definite time each day for your Bible reading.* Too often Bible reading is not done on a regular basis and we become discouraged when we can't remember what we have read or when we last read. It is better to set yourself a reasonable goal and stick to it than to read for long but irregular periods and become discouraged.

3. *Try to read at least a chapter at a time.* Bible readers often make the mistake of reading only a verse or two at a time. Sometimes this makes it impossible to understand what the Bible is about. Besides, it takes too long to read a single book of the Bible in this manner. Always try to read at least one chapter in a sitting and then ask yourself questions about what you have just read. Try to remember who was writing to whom, what was said, and why.

4. *Have a special place to read.* There is no use trying to read the Bible in front of the television set or while others are around you.

5. *Don't be disturbed if you don't understand all that you read.* Be sure to write down things that you are uncertain about and ask your parents or minister questions that come to you in your reading.

6. *Make notes as you read.* It is a good idea to write down your readings in a notebook so that you can look back over some weeks of reading and see what you have read. Some people keep such records for years!

7. *Try not to read the Bible just in emergencies.* The Bible is not just a "shelf of medicines" to be used at special times but "daily food" for all occasions.

8. *Try to have a regular devotional life, in addition to your Bible reading.* You should have a period set aside for your daily prayers. A good time for this is when you begin your Bible reading.

C. Scriptures for Specific Occasions

Although we have insisted that you should not *just* read the Bible on special occasions, there are a number of helpful and exciting chapters in the Bible which may be especially meaningful at certain times.

1. **When you are in doubt: Micah 6:6-8; 1 John 4:7-21**
2. **When you are choosing a life work: Matthew 25:14-30**
3. **When you need courage and strength: Psalms 27, 46; Ephesians 6:10-20**
4. **When you are setting out on a good time: Philippians 4:8-13**
5. **When you are lonely or fearful: Psalm 23**
6. **When you have done something wrong: Psalm 51**
7. **When family problems arise: John 15:9-17**
8. **When you are discouraged: Psalms 42, 43, 130**
9. **When you have failed: Psalms 27, 61**

   10. When you are happy: Psalms 96, 98, 150
   11. When death comes: Revelation 21:1-7; 1 Corin-
       thians 15:49-58

   Finally, remember that these are only suggestions. The best
thing for you to do is read the Bible. As important as it is to
have good books about the Bible, it is more important that you
not take any book as a substitute for the Bible. Read it and
find out what a treasure God has given us in the Bible.

9

THE LIFE OF
THE CHRISTIAN

Studying the Bible is important. So is telling others about Jesus. But these are only part of what the Christian life is all about. The way we respond to what God has done in Jesus only begins when we repent of our sin and are baptized into him. We then have the task of living a life that reflects the love of God in Jesus.

This task is not always easy. Sometimes Christians are faced with problems they can't solve and questions they can't answer. They may become very confused and discouraged. They face temptations to sin. This is why it is a good idea for every Christian to take a good look at himself when he first becomes a Christian. We need to try to understand just what sin is, why it causes guilt, and how and why God is willing to forgive us. Then, when problems arise later—and they will, no matter who we are—we will understand them and be better able to work through them.

A. Sin

Sin is real for all of us, since we each have different weaknesses and temptations. But sin is more than a single wrong act; it is a general condition that infects all men and is then seen in particular, sinful acts. One way of describing this state of sin is that it is alienation (separation or isolation) from God.

The Bible tells us that such a condition is not brought about by God but by man himself. Paul, when writing to the Christians in Rome, spoke of the Gentiles of past times who "although they knew God they did not honor him as God or give thanks to him, but they became futile in their thinking and their senseless minds were darkened" (Rom. 1:21). Paul goes on to say that because men first turned from God, he allowed them to follow the evil paths they chose (vs. 24).

The sad state of those without God is described by the prophet Amos, who speaks of those from whom God has withdrawn himself:

> They shall wander from sea to sea,
> and from north to east;
> they shall run to and fro, to seek
> the word of the Lord,
> but they shall not find it.
>
> Amos 8:12

The "running to and fro" well describes our situation without God. We become like a ship without a rudder, aimlessly tossing on the waves. This state of being without God is the state of sin.

Sin is man's tendency to place himself above God and others. Sin is a denial of God—it is atheism. It may be formal atheism, which leads one to say that God does not exist; or it may be practical atheism, in which one says he believes in God but lives as if God did not exist.

To deny God, either formally or practically, is to have a muddy and unclear view of life. Paul says that those who deny God are "futile in their thinking" (Rom. 1:21); they don't understand the real meaning of life. That is why their lives are

full of sins—the sins we often see in ourselves and others. So the root of sin is placing our own will above the will of God.

Sin thus confuses our outlook and leads to foolish and tragically wrong actions. Like a dog chasing a butterfly over a cliff, we are often led by sin to forget all the things that really matter, such as family, friends, and self-respect. Part of the cure or remedy for sin, therefore, is found in treating sin on this level. It consists of getting a new outlook—a new sense of what is important and what is not. Too often we fail to get to this deeper level of our sin, and we try to treat only the particular sin symptom. This way we may stop doing some single wrong things, only to find that sin shows its ugly face in some other part of our lives.

B. Guilt

One of the most frightful things about sin is the guilt it makes us feel. Each of us knows something about what it is like to feel guilty. We can understand the sad cry of David in the Bible:

> For I know my transgressions,
>   and my sin is ever before me.

Against thee, thee only, have I sinned,
    and done that which is evil in thy sight,
so that thou art justified in thy sentence
    and blameless in thy judgment.
Behold, I was brought forth in iniquity,
    and in sin did my mother conceive me.

Psalm 51:3-5

But we need to recognize that feeling guilt may be both good and bad. It may help us, or it may lead us further into sin. The sense of guilt comes when we feel we ought to do or not do something, or to be or not be a certain way. Then we recognize that we fail to meet up to what we ought to do or be. One way to deal with guilt is simply ignore it or deny it. If we do, we run the risk of doing great damage to ourselves spiritually, psychologically and even physically.

We need to recognize that nothing is gained by ignoring our feelings of guilt. We should examine them closely and try to understand why we feel this way. We may find that our feeling was based upon false information or a misunderstanding. In other words, we may find that we are not really guilty. In this way examining our feeling of guilt may lift a great burden.

Often, however, we find something else. We may painfully discover that we are indeed guilty or responsible for something wrong—perhaps something that has even hurt others. At this point, guilt may again have either a good or a bad effect.

If we allow our feelings of guilt to paralyze or cripple us into doing nothing, they do not help us. We may feel that our guilt is so great that there is no hope, no way that we can ever be free from the burden. Or we may decide that it is really too late ever to be free or forgiven and that the only thing to do is to continue in sin. A person who decides this is doomed to a miserable, lonely life.

On the other hand, guilt can be a useful tool that leads us to corrective action. If after a close examination we discover that our guilt is real, we must then try to remove it. The Bible, however, plainly teaches that we cannot remove our own guilt. Many people have gone through life trying to "wash off" or "work off" their guilt through endless acts of forced love and charity.

C. Forgiveness

The Bible teaches that God is a God who forgives sin. He alone can completely remove our guilt. Only by turning to God and trusting him to remove our guilt  can we truly have the freedom to live happy lives. God does not want us to feel guilty. He wants us all to have a new, free, and meaningful life that is without guilt. He alone can give this life to those who will let him heal them.

It is because of his desire that we come close to him and have this kind of life that God sent his Son to live among men. In Jesus Christ, God has established a new covenant with men. He wants all men to enter into this covenant and have new life through forgiveness of sin.

In order to accept Jesus as God's Son and have forgiveness of our sin, we must first repent. This means that we accept responsibility for the wrong in our lives and say that we are sorry that we have led selfish, willful lives.

Repentance means that we change our minds about wanting to live in sin, and turn our minds to the good, instead. It means changing our whole way of life—not that we expect to be perfect, but that we had now *rather* do right than wrong. Then we are baptized into Jesus. Our baptism is the way we show that we want God to "wash away" our sin and guilt, and to replace them with a new life in Christ.

We are not alone in trying to lead this new life, the Christian life. We have the Bible as a guide to help us, and we have the friendship and help of other Christians, our new family. But we have even more than this. God has promised that his Spirit will live in us and give us strength to reject sin.

D. Why Some Christians Drift Away from Christ

It is an unhappy thought that after making a new covenant with God and being baptized into Christ some Christians should drift back into lives of sin. But unfortunately it is true.

There are many reasons why Christians sometimes become disinterested and lose faith in Christ. Probably the most frequent problem is that we too often find that we weren't really converted to Christ in the first place. We discover that what we have thought of as "Christianity" was really something else. We find that we never really grew in faith because we got off on the wrong foot from the start. Perhaps we were rushed into conversion by some well-meaning friend. Or maybe we ourselves are responsible for being only partly converted. Either way, it often seems that we drift away because we never really got started.

If this is the case, we need to take another look at our baptism and conversion and make sure that we understand what life in Christ really involves. This can be an exciting period of discovery for us, and an important one. It is often helpful in such a task to talk with some other Christian, perhaps a minister, who can help us to reach a better understanding.

Another problem is that of "idols." Many Christians discover that their lives are empty in spite of their involvement in church. They turn to other concerns to fill spiritual needs —clubs, friends, or careers. These things may soon come to displace Christ and become "idols" just as dangerous as any ancient false idol. When we are guilty of following these false gods, we need to examine why we felt that they were important enough to replace Christ. What did they offer us? Whatever answers we find, they will help us understand how we have allowed Christ to be forced out of our lives.

Placing total loyalty in someone other than Christ is another problem that can hurt Christians. Like other people, Christians are often in search of a hero. While having heroes is not bad in itself, human beings can steer our goals and loyalties in the wrong direction. We can actually place heroes on a higher level than God.

All heroes—even preachers, teachers, elders, and other Christians—have weaknesses like people everywhere. They may be trying to do right as they understand it, but all make mistakes and face temptations. If we suppose they are perfect, we do them an injustice and hurt ourselves as well. Our hope and trust should be in Christ, not in men.

Christians sometimes fool themselves about why they drift away from Christ. Sometimes we do something and only later realize that our real reasons were not at all what we thought they were. We can find excuses to leave the church or weaken our love for Christ and say such things as, "Nobody cares about me anyway." Or we may tell ourselves, "I'll find a different church (or class)—one that is more helpful to me." Or we may dislike a certain sermon or class and then excuse stopping our attendance because of "bad" sermons or classes. We really are just looking for an excuse to do something we wanted to do for other reasons.

Finally, many people drift away from Christ simply by putting off doing what they know to be right. It is very easy for us to put things off. We feel that we have plenty of time. It is especially tempting for young people to think that they will have more time for pleasing God later on. Very often we feel that right now we just don't have time for God and church. We should realize how hard it is to break bad habits.

Coaches of all sports—tennis, swimming, baseball—agree that it is harder to teach a boy or girl the right way to do something if he has learned and practiced it wrong for a long time. It is the same way with our lives before God. We need to be careful not to develop careless habits, thinking that we can simply change them later.

We have looked at only a few of the more unusual ways that Christians drift away from Christ. There are many more, but, generally speaking, when a Christian has drifted from Christ, it is because he has been fooling himself in some way. This is why it is so important to examine ourselves closely when we first become Christians. Do we really understand the grip that sin has on our lives and how it can separate us from God? Do we really repent—really turn from our old life?

The life of the Christian can be an exciting adventure, with meaning and purpose that life could never have otherwise. So, even though our baptism is only the beginning of the journey, it is an extremely important step that must be taken with complete seriousness.

10

ARCHAEOLOGY AND THE BIBLE

Archaeology is the study of what people who lived in the past left behind them. The word *archaeology* means "study of beginnings." Geology is similar to archaeology, because it also studies the past and does so by digging in the earth. But geology is different because it studies rocks and minerals and is interested in the history of land formations. Archaeology is interested in things like buried pottery and buildings which will help us to understand the history of ancient men.

As a field of study, archaeology is newer than most sciences, having been studied less than two hundred years. It is limited because it can only study what survives for many centuries. Think how many buildings are torn down and totally destroyed each year. Like them, most of the things ancient people made and built have not survived. What does survive is not necessarily the best or most complete things that a people made. For example, a great piece of art may be destroyed and an unimportant plate survive.

A. Archaeology's Importance to the Bible

The Bible records the history of God's people. Because the Bible deals with people in history—in a particular time and place—that history is important. There are a number of ways archaeology can help us understand the Bible better.

First, archaeology can tell us something about the events and lives of people who lived before written history. Archaeologists have shown us what life was like in the country called Ur, where Abraham lived before God called him.

Second, Bible history can be made more complete with the help of archaeologists. For example, the Bible records only about fifteen verses about King Omri of Israel in 1 Kings 16. But from archaeology we learn that Omri was a very important king in his time.

Third, archaeology helps in translating and explaining many passages in the Bible that are hard to understand. For example, the Bible tells us that Rachel took the teraphim of her father Laban. For many years people did not know what teraphim were. But now archaeology has let us know that teraphim were small household statues, idols of false gods. In Laban's time, some people believed that the one who possessed them was the real owner of the family property.

Finally, archaeology has corrected false opinions that Bible history is untrue or imaginary. It has proved the truth of many things recorded in the Bible.

B. How Archaeological Finds Are Made

There are some outstanding discoveries which have been made by archaeologists, such as ancient temples in Egypt and Greece. Most archaeological discoveries, however, are small items found among city ruins. In ancient times, whenever a city was destroyed, the new inhabitants leveled off the old city and built another on top of it. After hundreds of years, several levels of ruins were piled on top of one another. These ruins, piled up in mounds, are called *tells*. Archaeologists dig up and examine material from different levels of these tells and learn about the people and their way of life at different times in the city's past.

Archaeologists find many important things in these ancient city locations. Old coins identify the time that the city existed, and metals in use at that time. Coins also give information about rulers because of the pictures and names on them. Clay pots and jars are significant, too, in dating the life of the city. And because paper was so rare in ancient times, pots were frequently used to write upon. In addition, archaeologists often find art objects, such as statues, idols, and carved pictures, which tell very much about ancient life.

C. Some Significant Archaeological Finds

There have been a large number of discoveries which relate to the Bible in the last two hundred years. To illustrate how these discoveries help in the study of the Bible, we will look at a few examples. These examples do not include some of the most significant finds, ancient manuscripts which have helped greatly in translating the Bible.

Abraham's ancestors. The list of Abraham's relatives in Genesis 11:10-26 contains many names that are not mentioned anywhere else in history. Before some significant archaeological discoveries were made, many felt that the names had some secret meaning. But archaeology has shown that these names can be traced to actual cities and people from the land around Haran where Abraham first traveled with his family.

Solomon's stables. While everyone knows that David was the great king of Israel, it was his son Solomon who ruled when Israel was a major nation in the ancient world. In the book of 1 Kings, we are told of the size of Solomon's chariot army (see 1 Kings 9:19; 10:26). This description has been made more certain with the investigation of the ancient city of Megiddo. There archaeologists have found a stable area that would hold five hundred horses, and chariots to go with them.

The tunnel of Siloam. In 700 B.C. the king of Israel, Hezekiah, built a large underground tunnel to get water to the city of Jerusalem during the seige (2 Kings 20:20). This project, only barely mentioned in the Old Testament, was confirmed by the discovery of the tunnel and a carving by the original builders of the tunnel to explain and mark the project.

The courtyard of Antonia. One of the archaeological discoveries which affects New Testament history is the courtyard of Antonia. Herod, the Jewish ruler, rebuilt an old fortress and named it Antonia (for the Roman ruler, Marc Antony). This became the military headquarters for the Roman governors of Judea. In the gospels, we learn that Jesus was tried at a place called "The Pavement" (John 19:13). It was not clear just what sort of place this was until archaeologists uncovered an area that fits this description. It was a courtyard made of large stones, perhaps where Roman soldiers were stationed. The stones have been marked where the soldiers played games.

The unknown god. In a sermon which Paul preached in the ancient Greek city of Athens, he referred to an altar "to an unknown god" (Acts 17:23) that had been built by the citizens. Some ancient Greek literature had confirmed that such a phrase was used by Greek poets. But archaeologists discovered an altar at the city of Pergamum which has the same inscription. This tells us that Athens was not the only pagan city to have such an altar.

D. The Dead Sea Scrolls

One of the most exciting archaeological discoveries related to the study of the Bible is the Dead Sea Scrolls found in 1947. The Dead Sea is the largest body of water in Palestine. Near this sea are the ruins of a former small village called Qumran (koom-RAHN) which existed from about 100 B.C. to A.D. 100.

Hidden in the caves among the ruins of this old location, archaeologists discovered a few complete books and thousands of fragments written by the ancient inhabitants. These writings are called the Dead Sea Scrolls. The people who began the community of Qumran were Jews who left Jerusalem about 100 B.C. to study the Law and wait for God to send a new leader like Moses. These people and their followers are frequently called Essenes. They are important because they give us information about ideas and practices which were present among Jews during the lifetime of Jesus. These documents also tell much about the vocabulary and way of life of the first Jewish Christians.

The Dead Sea Scrolls are also important because they tell us a great deal about the writing of the Old Testament. The people who lived at Qumran made many copies of the Old Testament books. In fact, some part of every Old Testament book except Esther has been found. These copies are the oldest copies of the Old Testament we have in the original Hebrew language. This helps translators of the Bible to work more accurately.

11

GREAT BIBLE DOCTRINES

In this chapter, we will examine some of the great teachings of the Bible. All of these are words that occur many times in the Bible and in studies of the Bible. Sometimes we read them so often that we don't really think about what they mean, and this can be dangerous if we have started with a false or unclear notion of their meaning.

Even if we think we have a pretty good idea of what some of these terms mean, it is a good idea to look back closely at them from time to time, because it is always possible to learn something more about them or to enrich our present understanding.

A. Baptism

The word "baptism" comes from a Greek word, *baptizo* (bap-TIDZ-oh) which means "to dip or plunge" something or someone under water. Early Christians were baptized, or dipped in water, upon acceptance of Jesus Christ as God's Son. Baptism is practiced in obedience to Jesus' command to baptize (Matt. 28:16-20).

Baptism is the way in which we give ourselves to God, saying with our actions that we will not live our lives selfishly but that we will live them as Christ wants us to. Four important things happen at baptism. First, God removes our sins. The guilt of past wrongs is forgiven—washed away—in baptism (Acts 2:38). Second, God's  Holy Spirit, the same Spirit that raised Jesus from the grave (see Resurrection and Holy Spirit), comes to live in us (Rom. 8:11; Acts 2:38). The Spirit, living in the Christian, helps him in his daily life, giving him strength not to sin and aiding him in his prayers to God (Rom. 8:26). Third, at baptism God's Spirit joins the baptized person to the church. It becomes his new family of brothers and sisters. Fourth, baptism is called a "new birth" (and the Christian a "new creation," 2 Cor. 5:17) not only because the baptized person is born into a new family but also because he begins life again at baptism. In this sense, it is important to see that baptism is not an end but a beginning of the Christian's exciting new life with God and man.

B. Christ

The word "Christ" comes from the Greek word *christos,* which means "anointed" (see *Messiah*). We see this word at work when, for example, a new ship is launched and is "christened." In ancient times, kings and other great men were anointed (1 Sam. 10:1; 16:1, 13) to show that they had been especially chosen by God. Jesus is called the Christ because he is God's chosen Son through whom God saves the world (Acts 10:38).

C. Church

The church is a group of people gathered by God. The church is not a building, although we sometimes speak of the building where Christians gather to worship as the church house or just "the church." The church was started by Christ and serves him (and so serves God) by preaching the gospel, worshiping, helping others, and living loving lives.

D. Covenant

"Covenant" is a word describing an agreement between two parties. In a covenant the people involved promise to be loyal to each other and to commit themselves not only to keep their promise to each other but also to honor the other person at all times in thought, word, and deed. For example, marriage is a covenant between two people where promises are made to be kept for life. And just as a man and woman give each other rings to show that they have made a covenant, people who entered into covenants in the Bible usually made some outward sign of the agreement. On one occasion a pile of large stones was built to show that two men had made an agreement or covenant (Gen. 31:46-47).

Covenants are made not only between people but also between men and God. Covenants with God also involve outward expressions of the agreement. For example, special meals were often eaten to express covenants or agreements with God (Ex. 24:3-11).

The two divisions of the Bible—the Old and New Testaments—actually refer to two different covenants that

God made with men (2 Cor. 3:6-18). Through Moses, God made a covenant with the Jews. Through Jesus, God has made a new covenant with us, forgiving us of our sins and calling for us to love and obey him. Signs of this covenant are the Lord's Supper and baptism.

E. Creation

The Bible tells us that God created the heavens, the earth and all that is on it, and men (Gen. 1, 2). Since God created it, the earth is good. As long as it is used in the way God intended, it remains good. The fact that God created all things also tells us that God is not in the stars or mountains as many primitive people believed. God made all things, and so he is apart from them. Further, all things belong to God. God made man to help him take care of the creation, to use and protect it in the way God wants.

F. Crucifixion

The word "crucifixion" comes from a word which means a cross. Crucifixion is the way Jesus willingly suffered the punishment for the sins of all men. The crucifixion shows the love which God and Christ have for us, a love so great that it was willing to suffer undeserved pain and death. The crucifixion is part of the Christian good news (see *Gospel*) because it tells of God's great love and forgiveness.

G. Faith

Faith is one of the central ideas of the Bible. The word "faith" has two important meanings that go hand in hand — trust and loyalty. That is, having faith in someone means trusting and having confidence in him, and also showing allegiance or loyalty to him.

We may understand faith better if we think about the relationship between children and their parents. Children can trust their parents because they know their parents love them. A small child may not understand why he cannot play in the street, but he will obey his parents because he has faith in them. And we may not always understand God's will, but we know that he loves us and we trust him and will be loyal to him.

We may also speak of "*the* faith." Used in this way, "the faith" refers to the truth which God has given us (Jude 3).

H. Gospel

This word means "good news." The Christian gospel is the good news of what God has done for us through his Son, Jesus. Jesus has shown us God's love through his life and death on the cross as he died for our sins (see *Crucifixion*). His resurrection (see *Resurrection*) further shows us God's power and love which wins over sin and death. The gospel is good news because it tells us that God loves us, forgives us, and will also raise us from the grave to live with him forever.

I. Grace

The word "grace" may be understood as "loving kindness." Grace is used to describe the way God loves us. God's grace is clearly seen in the fact that although men have been ungrateful and turned against him, God has continued to love men. We could say that God's grace is undeserved love. God loves us although we do not deserve his love.

Yet the proof of God's amazing love is this: that it was while we were sinners that Christ died for us.
Romans 5:8

God's grace is even more astonishing when we realize that he does not love us because we are good or deserving. He loves us so that we might become good. The whole Bible is the story of God's grace, his faithful loving-kindness. The high point of this story is Jesus' death (see *Crucifixion*), where God's grace is clearly seen: 'God loved the world so much that he gave his only Son . . ."(John 3:16, *New English Bible*).

J. Holy Spirit

The Holy Spirit is the power by which God does many of his great deeds. It was through the Spirit that God created the universe (Gen. 1:2). The great leaders of Israel—judges, kings, and prophets—were all given power and directions by God's Holy Spirit. But the Holy Spirit was especially at work in the life of Jesus, in his teaching and many mighty miracles. It was the Spirit of God who raised Jesus from the grave (Rom. 8:11).

The Spirit does many things in the church today. He works when the good news (see *Gospel*) is preached (1 Thess. 1:5; 1 Cor. 2:4). And the Spirit is at work when a person is baptized (see *Baptism*), joining him to the church and coming to live in him. The Spirit also gives strength and wisdom to the church and dwells in Christians, helping them live as God wants them to (Eph. 3:16).

K. Lord's Supper

As national holidays honor and remind us of special events, the Lord's Supper is a memorial meal in which Christians remember important events in the past. Jesus, the night before his crucifixion, ate a meal with his followers (called the "last supper") and commanded them to remember his death through a meal (1 Cor. 11:23-26). Christians today eat the Lord's

Supper in obedience to Jesus' request, remembering his death on the cross. The bread represents Jesus' body and the wine or grape juice represents his blood. These events are remembered because it is through them that God has forgiven us and created the church.

Three more points are important. First, the Lord's Supper looks back not only to Jesus' death. We eat it together on the first day of the week (Acts 20:7)—the day Jesus was raised from the grave (see  *Resurrection*). We know that Jesus was raised and still lives, and in this meal we celebrate his resurrection as well as his death.

Second, Christians eat the Lord's Supper together. We are God's family and love one another (1 Cor. 10:17).

Third, when we eat the Lord's Supper we look forward to the time when Jesus will return and be with his family (1 Cor. 16:22).

L. Love

Love is the basis of the Christian faith. God himself is love (1 John 4:8) and has shown that he loves us by the life and work of Jesus Christ (1 John 4:9-10). Jesus showed God's love because he was willing to give something, even his life, for our good (Rom. 5:6-8). Since we have been so loved by God and Jesus, we should love other men (1 John 4:11). In fact, this is the most important job we have (Rom. 13:8-10; 1 Cor. 13:1-13). But love is not simply a feeling, like the joy we have in families and with pets. Love is how we act toward other people. In this sense, love is being kind and helpful. It is doing to other people what we would want them to do for us (Luke 10:25-37).

M. Messiah

"Messiah" is a Hebrew word meaning "anointed one" (see *Christ*). In the Old Testament, priests, prophets, and kings were all anointed to their work by God. The term "Messiah," however, later came to refer to the one expected to come bringing God's peace and salvation to all men. The New Testament tells us of the coming of the long-awaited anointed one, or Messiah. He is Jesus of Nazareth (Luke 4:16-21; Acts 4:17).

N. Prayer

Prayer is communication with God. Often people think of prayer as merely asking God for favors; but requests are only a part of prayer, just as they are only part of our conversation with our friends. Prayer also consists of praising God, thanking him, submitting to his will, and telling him our mistakes. Because he loves us, God wants us to talk with him. And because he loves us, he also answers our prayers.

O. Resurrection

The New Testament tells us that God raised Jesus from the grave after the crucifixion. The term "resurrection" refers to this event. The resurrection of Jesus took place on a Sunday, and it is for this reason that Christians gather to worship on Sunday, the first day of the week.

Resurrection also refers to that event to which all Christians look forward, their own resurrection from death. Because of the resurrection of Christ, Christians know that God will also raise them after death to live with him forever.

P. Sin

To sin is to turn against God and refuse to do his will. God, who created us, knows what is good for us. He loves us and only wants what is best for us. To sin is to ignore or forget this. Just as a flower becomes sick without water, we are hurt when we turn away from God, the source of life, and choose sin.

Q. Worship

Worship is serving. When we worship God, we serve him. We worship God in two ways. First, we are worshiping when we live as God wants us to every day and are pleasing to him (Rom. 12:1-2). Second, we worship God when we gather with our families or others to worship God by singing songs, reading the Bible, and praying to him.

12

Great Men and Women of the Bible

The Bible is the story of God's love and of his relationships with the people he created. A number of these people stand out for their greatness as we read the Bible. Perhaps it is the loyalty they show to God which makes them especially memorable. Sometimes it is the courage or the faith or the deep love that is seen in their lives.

This chapter contains some brief sketches about just a few of the great men and women in God's story. They are surely not the only great people of the Bible, and they may not be the most important ones. But they are all men and women who loved God and whose lives can teach us a great deal about what it means to be God's people.

These character sketches do not summarize the lives of these people. The Bible dictionary will tell you more about the facts of their lives, and Chapters 4, 5, and 6 may help you understand their places in the history contained in the Bible. The best sources for learning about their lives are the scripture references mentioned at the end of each section.

These descriptions are intended to help you understand why these people were dear to the heart of God. As you read about how they used their talents for God and permitted him to turn their weaknesses into strengths, you may also be able to see some of the possibilities for faith and service in your own life.

A. Abraham

Abraham will be remembered as long as people trust and worship God. As the father of the Hebrew nation, Abraham entered into a covenant agreement with God. He promised his faith and obedience in response to the continual care of God.

Abraham often had to stand alone in his belief and trust in God, and he also had to suffer. God told him to leave his home and family, and he willingly went. He challenged rulers, endured loneliness, and suffered through times of need as he traveled, but he never forgot his covenant with God. Everywhere he pitched his tent, he also built an altar to God.

Abraham's greatest test was God's demand that he sacrifice his son Isaac, for whose birth he had waited many years. Abraham knew that if Isaac died he would have no son to carry on the covenant with God, and no heir to whom he could pass on his great faith and knowledge of God. But still he faced this test bravely. And God spared both Isaac and Abraham in the face of Abraham's great faith.

Abraham talked often with God, and he did not hesitate to speak frankly. He asked God not to destroy Sodom and Gomorrah, and God listened and answered Abraham. It is important to remember that when Abraham protested to God, it was for the sake of others, not himself.

This same selflessness was seen in Abraham's hospitality and friendliness. When God made him a powerful leader, he used his influence for others and gave freely, welcoming strangers into his home.

Abraham's adventurous life was filled with challenges, but his greatest adventure was his encounter and life in covenant with God.

The story of Abraham is told in Genesis 11 – 25.

B. Joseph

The story of Joseph is one of the most exciting life histories in the Old Testament. It is almost like a roller-coaster ride with great highs and great lows, and with events following one another at great speed.

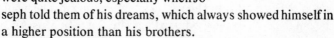

Joseph was the great-grandson of Abraham and the favorite son of his father, Jacob. His ten older brothers knew this well, because Jacob showed many special favors to Joseph. They were quite jealous, especially when Joseph told them of his dreams, which always showed himself in a higher position than his brothers.

God continued to provide for Joseph even after his spiteful brothers sold him into slavery. In Egypt, bad became worse when he was thrown into prison for a wrong he did not commit. But here Joseph interpreted the dreams of two fellow prisoners. When one of them was freed later, he remembered Joseph and brought him to the attention of Pharaoh.

In Pharaoh's court, Joseph became a favorite again. His talent and energy brought him fame and fortune instead of getting him into trouble. He showed himself to be a great organizer and to be honest, hard-working, and wise. And he also remained true to God's commandments, whether in high places or low. Through his faithful service and the blessings of God, the poor slave became a powerful, wealthy ruler, the Pharaoh's top adviser.

When Joseph was finally reunited with his brothers, their positions were reversed. He was the wise and mighty manager of Egypt's grain supply, and his brothers were poor foreigners, begging for relief from the long drought. It is a sign of Joseph's goodness that he received them with tears of thanksgiving, restoring them to brotherhood.

You can read about Joseph in Genesis 37 – 50.

C. Moses

No person in the Old Testament stands out as a greater, more powerful figure than Moses, the man who led God's people out of slavery and into nationhood. His task was huge. Through him, God changed history, so that nothing was ever the same for Israel after Moses.

Moses was born in a time of fear and slavery for the Hebrew people. His mother hid him as an infant, fearing that he would be put to death by the Egyptian Pharaoh. But baby Moses was found by Pharaoh's own daughter and brought into the palace to be reared as a prince. Part of Moses' greatness was his decision to give up his easy royal life and go out to his own people. He saw their suffering and he chose to come to their aid, even though it meant he had to flee Egypt and live in exile for many years.

When Moses returned to Egypt, it was not as a pampered prince but as a bold leader for the Hebrews. He stood up and told the mighty Pharaoh of God's will that his people be allowed to leave Egypt. After a stormy conflict and ten terrible plagues, Moses led God's people in the exodus from Egypt, across the sea to freedom. Soon afterward Moses received from God the law (the Ten Commandments) by which his people were to live.

Moses was sometimes short-tempered, and he complained of being a poor speaker. He was disturbed when the people were ungrateful to God and forgetful of his goodness. But Moses never failed to be faithful to God and to the law which he gave his people at Mount Sinai. He also remained faithful to

God's people, in spite of their faithlessness. He often defended them before God.

Moses' faithfulness called the people of Israel back many times to love of God and the keeping of his law. From Moses they learned what God wanted them to know about their duties to him and to one another. Moses' life teaches us the tremendous effect for good one strong and faithful person can have.

Moses' life and work are described in Exodus, Leviticus, Numbers, and Deuteronomy.

D. Deborah

Deborah was a woman of great faith who stepped into the history of Israel at a critical time. God's people had been led by Moses out of Egyptian slavery and by Joshua into the promised land, and then they had sadly forsaken God. They turned to other gods and lived evil lives. Deborah was one of the strong and faithful people, called judges, whom God raised up when his people began to forget him.

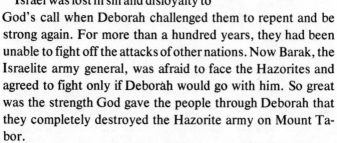

Israel was lost in sin and disloyalty to God's call when Deborah challenged them to repent and be strong again. For more than a hundred years, they had been unable to fight off the attacks of other nations. Now Barak, the Israelite army general, was afraid to face the Hazorites and agreed to fight only if Deborah would go with him. So great was the strength God gave the people through Deborah that they completely destroyed the Hazorite army on Mount Tabor.

"The Song of Deborah," a Hebrew poem found in Judges 5, tells of Deborah's vision and inspiring leadership. The new courage she brought to Israel helped the people regain the trust in God and the unity they had to have to be a nation. This unity was to grow still greater under the early kings.

Judges 4 – 5 tells the story of Deborah.

E. Ruth

Ruth was not born an Israelite. She was a young woman from Moab, a nation of people who were usually enemies to the Israelites.

But Ruth's devotion to her adopted country and family are part of one of the most beautiful love stories in the Bible. After her young Israelite husband died and his mother Naomi decided to return to Israel, Ruth told her mother-in-law that she wanted to go with her. Naomi protested that Ruth should stay with her own people in her own land. But Ruth answered with the touching words that have been long remembered and often repeated: "Where you go I will go, and where you lodge I will lodge; your people shall be my people, and your God my God."

In Israel, Ruth worked hard to make Naomi comfortable. Her kindness and dedication soon won the heart of Boaz, a wealthy man of Bethlehem who was related to Naomi's family. Ruth and Boaz married, and their son Obed became the ancestor of the great king David. Through David, Ruth herself became an ancestor of Jesus.

Ruth will always be remembered for her devoted care for and loyalty to Naomi. But most of all, the people of Israel treasured her courageous decision to leave her foreign gods and worship the God of the Israelites.

The book of Ruth tells the story of this great woman.

F. David

The second king of Israel — called the greatest in the nation's history — was a man of great heart. Everything he did, he did with enthusiasm. Sometimes this got him into trouble, but it also marked him for greatness.

As a boy, David was a shepherd. He made a name for himself while he was still very young when he came to visit his older brothers on the battlefield— and then killed with a slingshot the giant Goliath, of whom the whole Israelite army was afraid. David was soon taken into the court of Saul, where he became known for still other talents. He was a poet and a musician, and his music could soothe King Saul when nothing else could.

David with his good looks and likeable manner, was very popular in the king's court. But soon his talents and popularity made Saul jealous. Maddened by his envy and by David's many successes, Saul turned against his servant and tried to kill him. David was helped to safety by his best friend, Saul's son Jonathan.

When David became king in Saul's place, he showed his greatness in many ways. He was a courageous soldier and an inspiring leader. All his people loved him, and he helped the nation of Israel become stronger and more powerful.

David committed a terrible sin when he took Bathsheba for his wife and had her husband, Uriah, killed. But when Nathan the prophet accused him of this wrong, David freely admitted it, repented, and grieved deeply for his wrong. Though he sinned greatly, he also showed much devotion to God. He never undertook any task as a king without first asking of the Lord. Because of this, the scriptures call David "a man after God's own heart."

David's name is mentioned a great many times in both Old and New Testaments, but most of his story is told in 1 Chronicles 11 – 19.

G. Elijah

He came in from the wild country east of the Jordan River, where he lived and was fed by ravens. Boldly, this rough man confronted kings of Israel and Judah with harsh judgments on their sin. It was through the courage and outspokenness of Elijah the prophet that God made his will known for many years to the divided kingdom.

After David and Solomon, the country had become separated into two different kingdoms, and the people of both had turned away from God. For many years Elijah fearlessly faced the wicked kings of Israel and Judah and told them of the great shame they were bringing upon God's people. He boldly condemned King Ahab for his evil and selfishness, and he tirelessly struggled against the worship of the false god Baal.

One of the most dramatic encounters Elijah had with the Baal worshipers took place on Mount Carmel. Here he challenged the prophets of Baal to a contest to prove whether the Lord or Baal was God. Thousands of people watched as the 450 prophets screamed, cried, and begged Baal to send fire to the altar they had built. As the afternoon wore on and no answer came, their frenzy grew greater and they cut themselves with swords. But their efforts were all in vain. Then Elijah simply prayed to the Lord and fire fell and consumed the offering on his altar.

Yet this same strong and fearless man could also show great compassion and tenderness. A widow who shared her food with Elijah was provided with plenty to eat for her son and herself during a long drought in Israel. And when her son became ill and suddenly died, Elijah gently breathed into his nostrils until the boy was alive again.

The people of Israel remembered the boldness of Elijah and the miraculous way in which he was taken up to be with God.

Read about Elijah in 1 Kings 17 – 21 and 2 Kings 1 – 2.

H. Daniel

The most outstanding trait of the prophet Daniel was his loyalty to God. No matter what other people were doing, no matter even what the king decreed, Daniel continued to obey God's will.

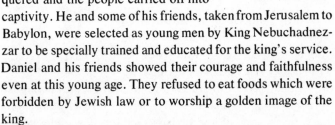

Because of his steadfastness, Daniel found himself in trouble often. But this same honesty and loyalty also caused him to be greatly honored by two kings, Nebuchadnezzar and Darius.

Daniel lived during the years after the divided kingdoms had been conquered and the people carried off into captivity. He and some of his friends, taken from Jerusalem to Babylon, were selected as young men by King Nebuchadnezzar to be specially trained and educated for the king's service. Daniel and his friends showed their courage and faithfulness even at this young age. They refused to eat foods which were forbidden by Jewish law or to worship a golden image of the king.

Later, when Darius became king, Daniel was given a position of honor. But other noblemen were jealous of Daniel and tricked King Darius into making a law against prayer to anyone but himself. When Daniel continued to pray openly every day to the Lord, he was thrown into a den of lions. The next morning, the king was overjoyed to see Daniel unharmed.

Because of the strong testimony of Daniel's life of trust and service, King Darius decreed that all the land should worship the God of Israel.

Daniel's strength when faced with a choice between disloyalty to God and death was no accident. Because he had for many years shown courage in the smaller choices of his life, he was ready for the great tests when they came. His story gave strength to the faith of the people of Israel during the sad years of exile.

Daniel's life is described in the book that bears his name.

I. Mary, Mother of Jesus

The young Jewish maiden who became the mother of Jesus stands out in the short Bible verses that tell about her for her goodness and obedience. We are told of a number of difficulties Mary suffered, but never of a lack of patience or faithfulness on her part.

Shortly after God's angel surprised Mary with the announcement of the coming birth of Jesus, Mary went to visit her cousin, Elizabeth. Elizabeth was soon to give birth to John who would become the Baptist. As the two shared their wonderful news with each other, Mary burst into a song of joy, praising God for the wonder he was soon to work through her.

Mary's life after the birth of Jesus was filled with wonder. She often found that she could not understand the things her son said and did, but she never ceased to be loyal and loving to him. At the temple in Jerusalem when Jesus was twelve, at

Cana of Galilee when Jesus turned water into wine, and on a number of other occasions Mary showed a strange mixture of puzzlement and joy. She had great faith in her son's ability and in God's promise, but often things that happened were simply beyond her understanding. Luke tells us that Mary "kept all these things in her heart."

Because Mary loved Jesus so much, she was at the foot of the cross when he was put to death. There Jesus gave his beloved friend John the charge of caring for Mary.

The last mention of Mary in the New Testament tells of her presence at a prayer meeting with the apostles and others following Jesus' resurrection and ascension. What complete joy Mary must have felt then, when all her hopes for her son had been gloriously realized and all her wondering brought to understanding!

Mary is mentioned in all of the four gospels. Read especially Luke 1 – 2 to learn about her life.

J. John the Baptist

John the Baptist had become well known in the area near the Jordan River before Jesus began his ministry. He must have been a strange sight, dressed in animal skins, eating wild food from the desert, and shouting fiercely against the people's corruption. His listeners asked if he were a prophet — he reminded them of the stories they had heard about Elijah — or perhaps the Messiah. But John said he was sent by God to prepare the way for the Messiah, who would be much greater than he.

John's warnings about God's coming judgment and about the need for repentance caused many people to be sorry for their sins. John baptized these people in the Jordan River, and he called on them to lead honest lives from that time on. But one day John's cousin Jesus appeared at the Jordan, asking to be baptized. At first John did not want to baptize Jesus, feeling that he was not worthy to do so. But Jesus convinced him it was God's will, and this baptism marked the beginning of his ministry.

Never fearful about pronouncing God's judgment, John got into serious trouble when he accused Herod, the Roman ruler of Palestine, of sinning by taking his brother's wife. Although Herod was furious at John's boldness, he was afraid to kill the prophet because of his reputation. So he put him in prison, where John stayed in solitude for a long time. At one time during his imprisonment he became so discouraged that he sent a messenger to Jesus to be sure he was the Messiah.

Toward the end of Jesus' ministry, John was beheaded by Herod. Jesus was deeply saddened when the news reached him. He went to a quiet place for a time to mourn the loss of this great man.

All four gospels tell about John the Baptist. Mark 1 and 6 are helpful references.

K. The Apostle John

"The disciple whom Jesus loved" is a name given to John in several places in the New Testament. Love is surely an important theme of the gospel of John and of the three letters written by John the apostle. It is no wonder that he is called the apostle of love.

And yet this same man, a fisherman who was the brother of James, was called by Jesus a "son of thunder." Perhaps this nickname came from the time he angrily suggested that Jesus call down fire from heaven on an unfriendly Samaritan village, or from the time he criticized a man who was not one of the twelve for healing in the name of Jesus. Also, he and his brother James, the other "son of thunder," once selfishly asked Jesus for a special place of importance when he came into his kingdom.

So John was an enthusiastic, vigorous sort of man who, like most people, was sometimes misguided. Yet he was one of the small group who was closest to Jesus, going with him to a number of places where the apostles as a group were not invited. There must have been much to love in this energetic, eager young man. And in his life is seen the possibility of transformation that so often is seen in those who were near to Jesus. He became a significant figure in the early church, often accompanying Peter on important missions.

John was probably the last of the twelve apostles to die. He lived to a very old age, serving the church in Jerusalem and later in Ephesus. During his later years he saw the church face many problems — quarrels, false teachers, lack of faith — and he always said that the answer to these problems was love — the same love seen in Jesus' life. John is believed to have died in exile on the Isle of Patmos after completing his last writing, the book of Revelation.

John is mentioned in each of the four gospels. Read also the book of Revelation and the three letters bearing his name.

L. The Apostle Peter

The life of the apostle Peter was a true adventure, a story of the great changes and growth that can occur within the life of a single person. Peter's given name was Simon, and this was what he was called when he was a fisherman by the Sea of Galilee. He was never a man to be idle or slow; he was outspoken, quick-tempered, and brash.

After he met Jesus many of these same qualities were often seen. Peter would speak out when no one else would, questioning Jesus and rebuking him freely. When six hundred soldiers came to arrest Jesus, Peter showed great bravery as he struck out with his sword to defend the Lord. But only hours later, perhaps struggling to understand why Jesus had refused his aid, he denied even knowing him.

It was when Peter came to understand Jesus' real purpose and the meaning of his cross that he became the strong Christian leader we read about in Acts. When Jesus gave him his new name, he was using a Greek word meaning "rock," and Peter's character was truly rock-like in the years to come. He preached the first Christian sermon on Pentecost, and through him God caused great things to happen in the early church.

Not long after the church had begun, Peter had a vision from God through which he came to know that God meant for the gospel to be for all. His visit to the home of Cornelius, a Gentile, opened the door for widespread preaching of the good news of Jesus to people of all nations and races.

History records that Peter was strong to the end, and that he died on a cross as his master had. His story tells us that the power of Christ is great enough to transform us into what God would have us to be.

Peter's life is told in all four gospels and in the book of Acts.

M. Martha and Mary of Bethany

The New Testament tells us that some of the closest friends Jesus had were two sisters and a brother who lived in Bethany: Martha, Mary and Lazarus. One of the  most exciting points in Jesus' ministry was his raising of Lazarus from death not long before his own crucifixion.

We are not told very much about Lazarus himself, but the writers of the gospels give us a glimpse into the kind of people his sisters were. Martha was a practical homemaker, always concerned about providing for Jesus' needs when he visited. Jesus appreciated her care, but was also a little sorry that such matters seemed so important to her. He once told her not to forget that some things were more important than household cares.

Mary was deeply devoted to Jesus, listening thoughtfully and intently to his words. In fact, she sometimes neglected to do her share of the housework when he was visiting because she was so keenly concerned with what he had to say. At one time she expressed her deep feeling for him by pouring precious oil on his feet and wiping it with her hair. Jesus praised her for understanding that the kingdom of God has a value above all other things.

Jesus loved both sisters, and he visited their home several times. When he came to see them after their brother's death, both expressed a deep faith in him. Meeting him at different times, they both spoke the same first words: "Lord, if you had been here, my brother would not have died." And before the day was over, Jesus had turned their grief to joy.

Read Luke 10 and John 11 – 12 to learn more about Martha and Mary.

N. The Apostle Paul

The apostle Paul was called by his Hebrew name, Saul, when he was growing up in Tarsus. While studying Jewish law in Jerusalem under the famous teacher Gamaliel, Paul became a dedicated Pharisee. His zeal led him to take part in the persecutions of early Christians and even in the stoning of Stephen.

But while Paul was traveling to Damascus to seek out other Christians, the risen Jesus appeared in a blinding light and asked, "Why do you persecute me?" Then Jesus told Paul that he was to be God's special messenger to the Gentiles. It would be hard to imagine anyone's life, thoughts, and actions being changed any more than Paul's were by that experience on the road.

When Paul did go on to Damascus, it was to preach to the Jews there, telling them that Jesus was the Messiah sent by God. Later the church at Antioch sent him out with Barnabas, Silas, and others on missionary journeys to many parts of Asia and Europe. During his travels Paul had many exciting adventures and encountered all kinds of people. He spoke before rulers, was jailed, beaten, shipwrecked, and finally imprisoned in Rome. He was probably put to death there by the wicked emperor Nero.

Paul's letters to the young churches he founded make up a large part of our New Testament. They have provided the church through the centuries with resources for making the gospel live through the Lord's people in every age.

Paul's writings show that he had a brilliant mind, that he held strong beliefs, and that he was a man of action. But what is important is Paul's life of deep commitment to Christ and his church, a life reflecting Christ's lordship.

Acts 8 – 28 tells the dramatic story of Paul.

PART TWO:
Important Verses From The Bible

This part of your Bible Handbook gathers into one section some very basic verses from the Bible. They can be used as a handy reference when discussions or questions send you to God's word for answers.

You may also want to begin memorizing these passages in a regular study program as many other young Christians have done. If so, here are some hints:

1. Memorize only one new verse at each session.

2. Set one or two short memory-work periods a day, instead of trying to study irregularly for longer periods. You may even want to jot down the passage on a card to carry around with you, referring briefly to it at free times during the day.

3. Review at least one of the previously learned verses at each session before tackling a new verse.

4. If possible, find a relative or friend who shares your interest. Study with them so that you can check each other's work.

5. Memorizing is usually easier when you write the verse several times, close your eyes, and try to picture the words. Use sight, hands, and ears all you can.

6. Don't forget how useless it is to memorize scriptures without understanding them. Ask for help if you have difficulty understanding the verse. Pray that this part of God's word will become a meaningful and applied part of your life, not just a part of your mind.

7. Watch for opportunities to use what you have memorized, without "showing off." Discussions in Bible classes and at home may give you a chance to reinforce what you have learned by repeating it. Perhaps several friends will join you in a club which has friendly memory-work competitions.

A. Baptism

Romans 6:3-4

Do you not know that all of us who have been baptized into Christ Jesus were baptized into his death? We were buried therefore with him by baptism into death, so that as Christ was raised from the dead by the glory of the Father, we too might walk in newness of life.

I Corinthians 6:11

But you were washed, you were sanctified, you were justified in the name of the Lord Jesus Christ and in the Spirit of our God.

I Corinthians 12:13

For by one Spirit we were all baptized into one body—Jews or Greeks, slaves or free—and all were made to drink of one Spirit.

Galatians 3:27

For as many of you as were baptized into Christ have put on Christ.

I Peter 3:21

Baptism . . . now saves you, not as a removal of dirt from the body but as an appeal to God for a clear conscience, through the resurrection of Jesus Christ, who has gone into heaven and is at the right hand of God, with angels, authorities, and powers subject to him.

Titus 3:5

He saved us, not because of deeds done by us in righteousness, but in virtue of his own mercy, by the washing of regeneration and renewal in the Holy Spirit, which he poured out upon us richly through Jesus Christ our Savior.

B. Church

Ephesians 1:22-23

And he has put all things under his feet and has made him the head over all things for the church, which is his body, the fulness of him who fills all in all.

Ephesians 5:23-27

For the husband is the head of the wife as Christ is the head of the church, his body, and is himself its Savior. As the church is subject to Christ, so let wives also be subject in everything to their husbands. Husbands, love your wives, as Christ loved the church and gave himself up for her, that he might sanctify her, having cleansed her by the washing of water with the word, that he might present the church to himself in splendor, without spot or wrinkle or any such thing, that she might be holy and without blemish.

Colossians 1:18

He is the head of the body, the church; he is the beginning, the first-born from the dead, that in everything he might be pre-eminent.

1 Timothy 3:15

If I am delayed, you may know how one ought to behave in the household of God, which is the church of the living God, the pillar and bulwark of the truth.

C. Confession

Matthew 10:32-33

So every one who acknowledges me before men, I also will acknowledge before my Father who is in heaven; but whoever denies me before men, I also will deny before my Father who is in heaven.

Romans 10:9-10

If you confess with your lips that Jesus is Lord and believe in your heart that God raised him from the dead, you will be saved. For man believes with his heart and so is justified, and he confesses with his lips and so is saved.

Philippians 2:9-11

Therefore God has highly exalted him and bestowed on him the name which is above every name, that at the name of Jesus every knee should bow, in heaven and on earth and under the earth, and every tongue confess that Jesus Christ is Lord, to the glory of God the Father.

1 Timothy 6:12

Fight the good fight of the faith; take hold of the eternal life to which you were called when you made the good confession in the presence of many witnesses.

Hebrews 10:23

Let us hold fast the confession of our hope without wavering, for he who promised is faithful.

D. Faith

Isaiah 26:3-4

Thou dost keep him in perfect peace,
whose mind is stayed on thee,
because he trusts in thee.
Trust in the Lord forever,
for the Lord God
is an everlasting rock.

Romans 5:1-2

Therefore, since we are justified by faith, we have peace with God through our Lord Jesus Christ. Through him we have obtained access to this grace in which we stand, and we rejoice in our hope of sharing the glory of God.

Hebrews 11:1-3

Now faith is the assurance of things hoped for, the conviction of things not seen. For by it the men of old received divine approval. By faith we understand that the world was created by the word of God, so that what is seen was made out of things which do not appear.

James 2:14-17

What does it profit, my brethren, if a man says he has faith but has not works? Can his faith save him? If a brother or sister is ill-clad and in lack of daily food, and one of you says to them, "Go in peace, be warmed and filled," without giving them the things needed for the body, what does it profit? So faith by itself, if it has no works, is dead.

E. Forgiveness

Matthew 18:21-22

Then Peter came up and said to him, "Lord, how often shall my brother sin against me, and I forgive him? As many as seven times?" Jesus said to him, "I do not say to you seven times, but seventy times seven."

1 John 1:9

If we confess our sins, he is faithful and just, and will forgive our sins and cleanse us from all unrighteousness.

Ephesians 4:32

Be kind to one another, tenderhearted, forgiving one another, as God in Christ forgave you.

James 5:15

The prayer of faith will save the sick man, and the Lord will raise him up; and if he has committed sins, he will be forgiven.

F. Grace

Ephesians 2:8-9

For by grace you have been saved through faith; and this is not your doing, it is the gift of God—not because of works, lest any man should boast. For we are his workmanship, created in Christ Jesus for good works, which God prepared beforehand, that we should walk in them.

G. Holy Spirit

1 Corinthians 2:10b-14

For the Spirit searches everything, even the depths of God. For what person knows a man's thoughts except the spirit of the man which is in him? So also no one comprehends the thoughts of God except the Spirit of God. Now we have received not the spirit of the world, but the Spirit which is from God, that we might understand the gifts bestowed on us by God. And we impart this in words not taught by human wisdom but taught by the Spirit, interpreting spiritual truths to those who possess the Spirit.

1 Corinthians 12:12-13

For just as the body is one and has many members, and all the members of the body, though many, are one body, so it is with Christ. For by one Spirit we were all baptized into one body—Jews or Greeks, slaves or free—and all were made to drink of one Spirit.

Galatians 5:22-23

But the fruit of the Spirit is love, joy, peace, patience, kindness, goodness, faithfulness, gentleness, self-control; against such there is no law.

Romans 5:5

God's love has been poured into our hearts through the Holy Spirit which has been given to us.

Romans 8:26-27

Likewise the Spirit helps us in our weakness; for we do not know how to pray as we ought, but the Spirit himself intercedes for us with sighs too deep for words. And he who searches the hearts of men knows what is the mind of the Spirit, because the Spirit intercedes for the saints according to the will of God.

H. Hope

1 Peter 1:3-4

Blessed be the God and Father of our Lord Jesus Christ! By his great mercy we have been born anew to a living hope through the resurrection of Jesus Christ from the dead, and to an inheritance which is imperishable, undefiled, and unfading, kept in heaven for you.

Romans 5:2-5

Through him we have obtained access to this grace in which we stand, and we rejoice in our hope of sharing the glory of God. More than that, we rejoice in our sufferings, knowing that suffering produces endurance, and endurance produces character, and character produces hope, and hope does not disappoint us.

Romans 8:24-25

For in this hope we were saved. Now hope that is seen is not hope. For who hopes for what he sees? But if we hope for what we do not see, we wait for it with patience.

Colossians 1:27

To them [the saints] God chose to make known how great among the Gentiles are the riches of the glory of this mystery, which is Christ in you, the hope of glory.

I. Lord's Supper

1 Corinthians 11:23-26

For I received from the Lord what I also delivered to you, that the Lord Jesus on the night when he was betrayed took bread, and when he had given thanks, he broke it, and said, "This is my body which is for you. Do this in remembrance of me." In the same way also the cup, after supper, saying, "This cup is the new covenant in my blood. Do this, as often as you drink it, in remembrance of me." For as often as you eat this bread and drink the cup, you proclaim the Lord's death until he comes. (See also Mark 14:22-25; Matthew 26:26-29; Luke 22:17-20.)

1 Corinthians 10:16-17

The cup of blessing which we bless, is it not a participation in the blood of Christ? The bread which we break, is it not a participation in the body of Christ? Because there is one bread, we who are many are one body, for we all partake of the one bread.

Acts 20:7

On the first day of the week, when we were gathered together to break bread. . . .

John 6:48-51

I am the bread of life. Your fathers ate the manna in the wilderness, and they died. This is the bread which comes down from heaven, that a man may eat of it and not die. I am the living bread which came down from heaven; if any one eats of this bread, he will live forever; and the bread which I shall give for the life of the world is my flesh.

J. Love

John 3:16

For God so loved the world that he gave his only Son, that whoever believes in him should not perish but have eternal life.

Romans 5:8

God shows his love for us in that while we were yet sinners Christ died for us.

1 Corinthians 13:7

Love bears all things, believes all things, hopes all things, endures all things.

Colossians 3:14

And above all these put on love, which binds everything together in perfect harmony.

1 John 3:18

Little children, let us not love in word or speech but in deed and in truth.

1 John 4:7-12

Beloved, let us love one another; for love is of God, and he who loves is born of God and knows God. He who does not love does not know God; for God is love. In this the love of God was made manifest among us, that God sent his only Son into the world, so that we might live through him. In this is love, not that we loved God but that he loved us and sent his Son to be the expiation for our sins. Beloved, if God so loved us, we also ought to love one another. No man has ever seen God; if we love one another, God abides in us and his love is perfected in us.

K. Obedience

John 14:15

If you love me, you will keep my commandments.

Hebrews 11:8

By faith Abraham obeyed when he was called to go out to a place which he was to receive as an inheritance; and he went out, not knowing where he was to go.

1 John 5:2

By this we know that we love the children of God, when we love God and obey his commandments.

L. Prayer

Matthew 6:6

But when you pray, go into your room and shut the door and pray to your Father who is in secret; and your Father who sees in secret will reward you.

Matthew 21:22

And whatever you ask in prayer, you will receive, if you have faith.

Romans 8:26

Likewise the Spirit helps us in our weakness; for we do not know how to pray as we ought, but the Spirit himself intercedes for us with sighs too deep for words.

1 Thessalonians 5:16-18

Rejoice always, pray constantly, give thanks in all circumstances; for this is the will of God in Christ Jesus for you.

Philippians 4:6

Have no anxiety about anything, but in everything by prayer and supplication with thanksgiving let your requests be made known to God.

James 5:16

Therefore confess your sins to one another, and pray for one another, that you may be healed. The prayer of a righteous man has great power in its effects.

M. Resurrection

1 Corinthians 15:20

But in fact Christ has been raised from the dead, the first fruits of those who have fallen asleep. For as by a man came death, by a man has come also the resurrection of the dead. For as in Adam all die, so also in Christ shall all be made alive.

Romans 4:24-25

It will be reckoned to us who believe in him that raised from the dead Jesus our Lord, who was put to death for our trespasses and raised for our justification.

Romans 6:5, 9

For if we have been united with him in a death like his, we shall certainly be united with him in a resurrection like his. . . . For we know that Christ being raised from the dead will never die again; death no longer has dominion over him.

Romans 8:11

If the Spirit of him who raised Jesus from the dead dwells in you, he who raised Christ Jesus from the dead will give life to your mortal bodies also through his Spirit which dwells in you.

2 Corinthians 1:9

Why, we felt that we had received the sentence of death; but that was to make us rely not on ourselves but on God who raises the dead.

N. Worship

John 4:23-24

But the hour is coming, and now is, when the true worshipers will worship the Father in spirit and truth, for such the Father seeks to worship him. God is spirit, and those who worship him must worship in spirit and truth.

Acts 20:7

On the first day of the week, when we were gathered together to break bread. . . .

Colossians 3:16-17

Let the word of Christ dwell in you richly, as you teach and admonish one another in all wisdom, and as you sing psalms and hymns and spiritual songs with thankfulness in your hearts to God. And whatever you do, in word or deed, do everything in the name of the Lord Jesus, giving thanks to God the Father through him.

Hebrews 10:25

. . . not neglecting to meet together, as is the habit of some, but encouraging one another, and all the more as you see the Day drawing near.

Romans 12:1

I appeal to you therefore, brethren, by the mercies of God, to present your bodies as a living sacrifice, holy and acceptable to God, which is your spiritual worship.

PART THREE:
Bible
Dictionary

Idol

ANGI

DEACON

HEAVEN FLOOD

JUSTIFICATION

Abraham

eace

TRANSLATE

entitude

Isaiah

CALVA

REPENTANC

A

Aaron (AIR-un) was the brother of Moses and Miriam. When God called Moses to help free his people from slavery in Egypt, Moses at first objected because he was too timid to speak before Pharaoh's court. God told Moses that he would use his brother Aaron as a speaker (Exod. 4:1-17). Together, Moses and Aaron went before the Pharaoh and finally got permission for God's people to leave Egypt. After Moses led the people out of Egypt, Aaron committed

a great sin while Moses was outside the camp. He allowed the people to build and worship a false god, an idol (Exod. 32:1-24). God forgave him, however, and when the tabernacle was built, Aaron and his sons were made priests (Lev. 8:1–9:22).

abba (AB-uh) was the Aramaic child's word for *father*. The fact that Christians can use this word to address the God of the universe shows the closeness of their relationship to him (Rom. 8:15; Gal. 4:6).

Abel (AY-b'l) was the son of Adam and Eve, the first man and woman. He offered God a lamb from his flock while Cain, his brother, offered God some of his crops. God accepted Abel's sacrifice but did not accept Cain's, and Cain killed Abel because of jealousy (Gen. 4:1-12).

Abiathar (uh-BY-ah-thar) was the son of Ahimelech, the high priest who was killed by King Saul for aiding David (1 Sam. 22). Abiathar escaped and joined David. Throughout David's reign, Abiathar was loyal to him. However, as David became old, Abiathar joined the rebellion of

Adonijah against David's son, Solomon (2 Sam. 15; 17:15; 19:11).

Abner (AB-ner) was the cousin of King Saul and the commander-in-chief of his army. He led forces against King David after Saul's death, but was defeated (1 Sam. 14–15). Later he came to join David, who forgave and received him kindly. But Joab, David's general, felt that Abner was a spy and murdered him.

Abraham (AY-bra-ham) was one of the greatest men of the Bible. The story of his call and his life of faithful obedience is found in Genesis 11–25. Abraham's name means "the father is exalted." His father was Terah and his wife was Sarah. Abraham was the founder of the Hebrew nation. God called him to move from his home to another land called Canaan (see map A), promising him in a vision that his children would inherit the land and that through his children and their children all men would be blessed.

God had promised Abraham that he would give him a son. But after a long time, Abraham and Sarah began to doubt whether God would bless Sarah with a son. So Abraham took another wife, Hagar, who had a son named Ishmael. Thirteen years later God told Abraham that he was still going to give him a son through his first wife, Sarah. When Abraham was a hundred years old, a son was born to Sarah. He was named Isaac. This was the promised son, the one from whom the Hebrew nation descended.

Although Abraham sometimes doubted God regarding the promise to give a son to Sarah, he is remembered for his great trust in God. The best-known story showing Abraham's faith is the one in which God asked Abraham to take Isaac up on a mountain and sacrifice him. Abraham was willing to do this although he loved his son very much. God did not let Abraham sacrifice his son. He only wanted to see how much Abraham really did trust him. It is because Abraham had so much faith in God that he is remembered as the "father of the faithful." (See also "The Call of Abraham," p. 32.)

Abram (AY-brum) was the original name of Abraham, before God changed it when he called him.

Absalom (AB-sa-lum) was the third son of David, the king of Israel, and a source of much grief to his father. Among other things, Absalom planned the murder of his older brother and fled his home for several years.  Finally David forgave Absalom and allowed him to return home (2 Sam. 13–14). Some years later, Absalom announced himself king and led a rebellion against his own father. In a battle with David's army, led by the ruthless general Joab, Absalom's long hair was caught in the branches of a tree as he rode beneath it. Joab and his men found Absalom there and, against David's orders, killed him (2 Sam. 15–18).

Achaia (uh-KAY-uh) was in New Testament times a Roman province which, along with Macedonia, included all of Greece. Paul visited a number of cities in this province during his missionary journeys (see maps F, G).

Achan (AY-kan) was an Israelite who disobeyed the order not to take anything from the ruins of Jericho after the battle there. He hid a garment and some gold and silver in his tent. This disobedience caused God to punish all of Israel by a defeat at Ai (Josh. 7).

Acts of the Apostles (See "History" p. 23; and ch. 6.)

Adam (AD-um) means "out of the earth" and is the name of the first man, created by God to care for the creation and to enjoy it (Gen. 1:26-30). Because Adam was the first man, "adam" is also the word used for *mankind* in the Old Testament. The first man was made in the likeness of God (see "Image of God"), but he rebelled and disobeyed God. Since sin entered the world with Adam, it has spread so that all men become sinners and are removed from the happiness for which God intended them. This barrier, however, has been overcome in the life, death, and resurrection of Jesus, the "Second Adam" (Rom. 5:14-21; 1 Cor. 15:22, 45).

adoption (uh-DOP-shun) in the Bible may mean what it does in common speech today. When a family takes a child and gives it the family name and full membership in the family, we say that the child has been adopted. This meaning is common to the Old Testament (Exod. 2:10; Esth. 2:7). However, in the New Testament the word is used to explain the relationship between Christians and God (Gal. 4:1-3; Rom. 8:1-15). God has adopted us, as Christians, as his own children and given us many joys and privileges. We should therefore be obedient and considerate children, thankful for what he has done for us (Eph. 1:4-12).

adultery (uh-DUL-ter-ee) refers to the practice of a man living with the wife of another man as if they were married to each other. It is forbidden in both the Old Testament (Exod. 20:14) and the New. In the New Testament it is seen as a special evil because it involves both body and soul.

advocate (AD-vo-kat) means *supporter* or *helper,* one who speaks for the cause of another. In the New Testament this term is used for Jesus (1 John 2:1-2) and the Holy Spirit

(John 14:26; 15:26; 16:7), both of whom are our advocates with God.

Agrippa (uh-GRIP-uh) was the name of two important people in the time of Paul. Agrippa I, also known as Herod Agrippa, was the grandson of Herod the Great and the king of the Jews at the time of Jesus' birth. Agrippa I ruled over Galilee, Judea, and Samaria. It was Agrippa I who had Jesus' brother, James, killed and the apostle Peter arrested (Acts 12:2-4).

Agrippa II was the son of Herod Agrippa and is referred to simply by the name Agrippa. He was the ruler before whom Paul gave his defense for becoming a Christian (Acts 25:23–26:32).

Ahab (AY-hab) was king in the northern half of Israel from 873 to 850 B.C. He was a strong ruler but is remembered for the evil which he did. Ahab allowed his wicked wife, Jezebel, who was not an Israelite, to build altars to false gods in the nation of Israel (1 Kings 18–19). Because of this sin and because he also murdered a man (Naboth) to get his vineyard, God allowed Ahab to be killed in battle (1 Kings 22:34).

Ahaz (AY-haz) was the twelfth king of Judah (735-715 B.C.). He ruled with his father for four years and then as king by himself for sixteen years. During his rule, many Israelites were carried into foreign captivity. Because of his treaties with other nations, Ahaz accepted the worship of idols as false gods and closed the Lord's Temple. Because of his wickedness, he was not buried with other kings of Israel (2 Chron. 28:24-25).

Ahimelech (uh-HIM-eh-lek) was Saul's high priest who helped David in his bid to become king. For this he was killed by Saul (1 Sam. 21–22).

Alexandria (Al-eg-ZAN-dree-uh) was a major city in Egypt built by the Greek king, Alexander the Great (see maps F, G). It was an important port city for ships carrying food and grain and also a great center of learning. It was in this city that a great deal of study of the Old Testament was done in ancient times. Later it was also a center of Christian preaching and writing.

alleluia (al-leh-LOO-ya) is sometimes written *allelujah, halleluia,* or *hallelujah.* It is a Hebrew expression meaning "Praise you the Lord." In the book of Psalms it is often found both before and after particular psalms. This use comes from the fact that the psalms were sung as praise to God in Temple worship. Alleluia is found in the New Testament in the book of Revelation (19:1, 3, 4, 6) and has continued to be used in Christian singing.

alms (ALMZ or AHMZ) are kind deeds done to those who need food, shelter, or other aid. Most frequently the giving of alms refers to giving money to the unfortunate. The giving of alms is taught by Jesus (Luke 11:41; 12:33), but he criticizes people who give to the poor in a show-off manner to gain the recognition of men (Matt. 6:1-4).

alpha (AL-fa) is the first letter in the Greek alphabet (a word which comes from *alpha*). The last Greek letter is *omega*, and sometimes the two letters are used together to signify completeness. Jesus is called "the Alpha and Omega" (Rev. 21:6; 22:13), as is his Father (Rev. 1:8). Today, we use the expression "A to Z" in a similar way.

Alpheus (AL-fee-us) is the name of the father of Levi or Matthew (Mark 2:14) and the father of the apostle James "the less" (Mark 3:18). It is likely these are two different men.

altar (AWL-ter) is a word used for a place of worship, and specifically for a place of animal sacrifice. Altars for sacrifice are very often mentioned in the Bible. They were made of many different materials such as stone, bronze, and wood. The first altar actually mentioned is that made by Noah (Gen. 8:20), although we suppose that Abel also had made an altar.

Much of the book of Leviticus deals with regulations about the design and use of the altar in the tabernacle. When Solomon built the Temple, it had a similar altar. The New Testament does not refer to altars other than those of the Jewish or Greek religions. This is because Christians do not offer animal sacrifices and thus have no need for altars.

Amalekites (ah-MAL-ek-ites) were ancient people living in the Negeb desert area from the times of Abraham to Hezekiah (see map A). They are often mentioned in the history of Israel (Exod. 17:8; Num. 14:45; 1 Sam. 15).

Ammonites (AM-un-ites) were a nation in Old Testament times who lived in Ammon (see maps, A, B, C). They often combined with another nation, the Moabites, to oppose Israel. There are several examples of the extreme cruelty they worked on Israel (1 Sam. 11:2; Jer. 40:17; 41:5-7).

Amos (AY-mus) was an Old Testament prophet and there is a book of prophecy bearing his name (see p. 18). He was a herdsman and a farmer when God called him to carry a message to the northern kingdom, Israel. This was unusual because Amos lived in Tekoa (see map C), a city in the southern nation, Judah.

Amos delivered the message, a warning of the coming destruction of northern Israel, at a temple supported by the king of Israel. The king and his friends then threatened Amos' life, which did not change the truth of his prophecy (Amos 7).

Ananias (An-uh-NYE-us) is the name of three men who played roles in the early church. One was an early Christian who, along with his wife Sapphira, deceived the church about a gift they were giving. They were punished by death for lying to the Holy Spirit (Acts 5:1-11).

Another Ananias was a Christian in Damascus who, in response to a vision, helped restore the sight of Paul (then called Saul) and brought him to the other Christians there (Acts 9:10-19).

The high priest before whom Paul was tried in Jerusalem was also named Ananias (Acts 23:1-5).

Andrew (AN-droo) was the brother of Simon Peter and also a fisherman on the Sea of Galilee. He was one of the special disciples of Jesus who were called apostles (Mark 1:23) and was also one of the four who heard Jesus give his teaching on the destruction of Jerusalem (Mark 13:3).

angel (AIN-jel): usually a heavenly being created by God just as man was (Gen. 1:31; Jude 6) but with a different type of life than man (Ps. 148:2-5). They are "spiritual beings" in the sense of not being human (Luke 20:24-36). The word basically means a *messenger*, and this is most often the function of angels in the Bible—they bring messages from God (Num. 22:35; Judges 13:12; Job 33:23).

A particular example is the announcement about Jesus' birth that was brought by an angel (Luke 2:8-15).

There are various ranks of angels. Michael is called an *archangel* (Jude 9) which means a ruler over angels. Some are evil angels (Ps. 78:49; Job 33:22). Good angels will be separated from the evil when God judges his created world (Matt. 25:41; Rev. 20:1-10).

"Angel of the Lord" is a frequent expression in the Old Testament. It refers to angels who are doing the work of God, perhaps as messengers, but sometimes as more than this (Gen. 16:7-14; Exod. 3:2-5; Judges 6:11-23).

Annas (AN-as) was a high priest of the Jews during Jesus' lifetime (Luke 3:2; Acts 4:6). Jesus was taken before Annas the night he was arrested (John 18:12-23).

anoint (uh-NOINT) means to pour oil on a person for a special purpose. It might be to show respect (Luke 7:46) or it might be to treat a body for burial (Mark 14:8; 16:1). But most often in the Bible it was a sign which set aside someone for a special task, such as to serve as a prophet, a priest, or a king (Exod. 28:41; 1 Sam. 9:16; 1 Kings 19:16). (See also "Lord and Christ," p. 49; and "Messiah," p. 96.)

antichrist (AN-tee-christ) means an enemy of Christ or one who tries to exercise powers that really belong to Christ as Lord (1 John 2:18, 22; 4:3; 1 John 7).

Antioch (AN-tee-ahk) is the name of two cities mentioned in the New Testament. One was the capital of Syria and was the home of the church where Christians were first called by this name. It was the first Gentile church and the one that sent out Paul and Barnabas on their first missionary journey.

The other Antioch was located in the province of Pisidia in Asia Minor. Paul and Barnabas preached in the synagogue there on their first missionary journey but were driven out by Jews jealous of their success (see maps F, G).

apocalypse (uh-POK-uh-lips) is from a Greek word meaning "disclosure" or "revelation." It is a name sometimes given to the New Testament book of Revelation (see "Prophecy," p. 27).

apocalyptic literature (uh-POK-uh-LIP-tik LIT-er-uh-tyoor) is writing that discusses such things as the secret purpose of God and the end of the world. It usually deals with the future and uses a great deal of *symbolism*. It is therefore often hard to understand. Examples of apocalyptic literature found in the Bible are the books of Daniel and Revelation.

Apocrypha (uh-POK-ri-fuh) refers to a collection of books written much like some of the books of the Bible and dealing with some of the same subjects. However, these books were not in the earliest Bibles. The books often included in modern collections of the Apocrypha are:

The First Book of Esdras
The Second Book of Esdras
Tobit
Judith
The Rest of the Chapters of
 the Book of Esther
The Wisdom of Solomon
Ecclesiasticus or the Wisdom
 of Jesus son of Sirach

Baruch
A Letter of Jeremiah
The Song of the Three
Daniel and Susanna
Bel and the Dragon
The Prayer of Manasseh
The First Book of Maccabees
The Second Book of Maccabees

apostle (uh-POS'l) means "one sent forth" and is the name given to the twelve men chosen by Jesus as his special disciples. These twelve were with Jesus during his earthly ministry, saw him after his resurrection, and laid the foundations of his church. After Judas betrayed Jesus to his enemies and then killed himself, Matthias was chosen by the eleven remaining apostles to take his place (Acts 1:15-26). Paul was later made an apostle as well, though he was not a follower of Jesus during his earthly ministry as the others were. Thus, the early church's list of apostles included Peter, Andrew, James the son of Zebedee, John, Philip, Bartholomew, Thomas, Matthew, James the son of Alphaeus, Simon the Zealot, Thaddeus, Matthias, and Paul (Matt. 10:2-4; Mark 3:14-19; Luke 6:13-16; Acts 1:13-26).

Though the apostles were closer to Jesus than anyone else during his lifetime, they had trouble understanding his mission and how he would carry it out (Mark 8:31-33). They did not expect his resurrection, as the gospels all tell us of their great surprise at seeing him alive after three days. But after they had seen Jesus raised and then had the experience of receiving the Holy Spirit on Pentecost they were changed men. They were ready to preach and teach powerfully and fearlessly and give their lives for the sake of Jesus and his church.

apostolic age (AP-os-TOL-ik) is that period in the history of the early church when the apostles were still alive. It lasted from the Day of Pentecost until the death of the apostle John about the end of the first century A.D.

Aquila (AK-wi-lah) was a Jewish Christian of Corinth, a tent-maker by trade. He and his wife Priscilla (or Prisca) were of great help to Paul in his ministry in Corinth, where he lived with them for some time and worked in their tent-making business (Acts 18:2, 18, 26). Aquila and Prisca had a church in their house (1 Cor. 16:19).

Aramaic (AIR-uh-MAY-ik) was a language closely related to Hebrew. It is likely that Jesus spoke this language during his life on earth. (See also "Languages of the Bible," p. 4.)

archaeology (are-kee-OL-oh-jee) (See ch. 10.)

ark is the name of a huge boat in which Noah and his family and the animals God told him to take into it floated during the great flood (Gen. 6–8). *The Ark of the Covenant* was a chest in which the tablets of the Law given to Moses were kept (Exod. 25:10-22). It traveled with the Israelites during their years of wandering (Num. 10:33) and rested in the tabernacle or the Temple in Jerusalem after it was built (2 Sam. 6; 1 Chron. 13; 15).

Armageddon (are-mah-GED-un) is a word used only once in the Bible (Rev. 16:16) for the scene of the final conflict between the forces of good and evil.

Artemis (ARE-teh-mis) was the Greek goddess of hunting, called Diana by the Romans. Paul preached against the worship of this false goddess at Ephesus, home of a great and famous temple built in her honor (Acts 19:23-41).

ascension (uh-SEN-shun) is the word for Jesus' return to be at the right hand of God after his death and resurrection (Luke 24:50-52; Acts 1:6-11).

Asher (ASH-er) was one of the twelve sons of Jacob and thus founder of one of the twelve tribes of Israel (Josh. 19:24-31; see map B).

Ashtoreth (ASH-toh-reth) was a goddess·worshiped by the Canaanites. At one time, the Israelites forsook God to worship her (Judges 2:11-23), but Samuel persuaded them to forsake this false worship and return to God (1 Sam. 7:3-4).

Asia (AY-zhuh) is the great continent east of Europe and Africa, which includes the world of the Old and New Testaments. Asia Minor is a western part of this continent where Paul traveled a great deal as a missionary (see maps F, G).

Assyria (uh-SEAR-ee-uh) was a powerful nation from the tenth to the seventh centuries B.C. (see map D). In the year 721 B.C., the Assyrians conquered the Northern Kingdom, Israel (2 Kings 17). (See also "Kingdom and Exile," p. 36.)

Athens (ATH-enz) was one of the leading cities of ancient Greece, now its capital (see maps F, G). Paul visited Athens on his second missionary journey and preached on Mars Hill (Acts 17).

atonement (uh-TONE-ment) means the repayment for or cancellation of a wrong. In the Old Testament, it meant the temporary covering cf sins by the blood of sacrificed animals. In the New Testament, atonement refers to the removal of all men's sins by the death of Jesus Christ (Rom. 5:11).

Atonement, Day of: a Hebrew celebration begun during the time of Moses. It was one of the seven great feasts of the Hebrew year. It was the only time of the year when the high priest entered into the holy of holies (see HOLY OF HOLIES). On this day, he offered sacrifices for the whole nation (Lev. 23:27; 25:9).

Augustus Caesar (aw-GUS-tus SEE-zer) or Caesar Augustus, was the reigning emperor of the Roman Empire from 31 B.C. until A.D. 14, which included the time of Jesus' birth and early life. The only mention of Augustus Caesar in the New Testament is Luke 2:1.

B

Baal (BAY-al) has a number of meanings in the Old Testament. It sometimes means a husband or the owner of a slave. But most often it refers to the local gods of nature in Canaan. These gods were worshiped at many places, frequently on top of hills (called the "high places"). Worship of the Baals was felt to insure good harvest of farm crops and large herds of animals. Because of the immorality of their worship, the Baals were often attacked by Israelite prophets (1 Kings 16:1; 18:36-40).

Baal-Zebub was a Philistine god (2 Kings 1:2-16). With some changes in spelling (Beelzebub), the word came to refer to Satan in the New Testament (see Matt. 12:24; Mark 3:22-23; etc.).

Babel (BAY-bel) is a name commonly used to refer to a tower men built on the plain of Shinar in Babylon in a vain attempt to see God (Gen. 11:1-9). It probably came to be used because the word meant "confused and unclear speech" (like our word "babble") and seemed to be a good description of the results of building this tower.

Babylon (BAB-ih-lon) is the name of both a country and its capital city in the Old Testament (see map D). The country was a very important power from about 700 to 500 B.C. and was well known for the beauty of the "hanging gardens" built by its king, Nebuchadnezzar. From 598 to 586 Babylon (or Babylonia) waged war on Jerusalem, which was finally destroyed (see "Kingdom and Exile," p. 36).

In the New Testament, Babylon is used as a symbolic name for the enemies of God, probably referring specifically to the Roman Empire (1 Pet. 5:13; Rev. 14:8).

Balaam (BAY-lam) was a magician hired by a prince of the country of Moab to place a curse on the people of Israel and thus keep them out of his land (Num. 22:1-6). But God caused Balaam to bless Israel instead (Num. 22–24). Later, he tried to persuade the Israelites not to worship God, and for this he was put to death (Num. 31:8). Because of his attempt to keep them from worshiping God, Balaam's name became used by the Israelites to refer to anyone who tried to lead God's people astray (Jude 11; 2 Pet. 2:15).

balm (BALM or BAHM) is a scented resin or gum which was highly valued for its ability to treat wounds (Jer. 51:8). This healing property is what is referred to in the phrase "balm of Gilead," which is sometimes heard in hymns.

baptism (BAP-tizm) in New Testament times usually referred to dipping converts in water to signify the forgiveness of sins and their initiation into the fellowship of believers.

A "baptism of fire" refers to a severe trial or persecution (Matt. 3:11; Mark 10:38-39).

The "baptism of the Holy Spirit" (Acts 1:5, 2:1-4) "immersed" the apostles in the power of the Spirit, and they were able to speak in foreign languages and perform miracles. (See also "Forgiveness," p. 79; and "Baptism," p. 89.)

Bar- is an Aramaic word which means "son." In the New Testament it is used in men's names. For example, the name *Bar-Jonah* (Matt. 16:17) means "son of Jonah."

Barabbas (bar-AB-as) was a criminal who was chosen for release instead of Jesus at the time of Jesus' trial. The gospel of Matthew tells us that he was a famous criminal (Matt. 27:16). The other gospels say that he was guilty of murder and robbery (Mark 15:7, 15; Luke 23:18-19; John 18:40).

Barak (BAYR-ak) was a Hebrew leader during the years when judges ruled Israel. He helped the prophetess Deborah win a battle against the Canaanites (Judg. 4:6 — 5:15).

barbarian (bar-BEAR-ee-un) at one time meant a person who did not speak Greek. Later, it came to refer to people who were not a part of the Roman Empire (Rom. 1:14; Col. 3:11).

Barnabas (BAR-nah-bus) was a Levite (a man of the priestly tribe of Levi) from the island of Cyprus. He is introduced in Acts 4:36 and later becomes a worker in the Christian mission effort with the apostle Paul. They worked together at Antioch (Acts 11:22-26) and on the first missionary journey (Acts 13–14). Barnabas went to the Jerusalem council with

Paul but later split with him over Paul's refusal to take Mark on the second missionary journey (Acts 15:12, 36-41). Paul's letters show that he thought very highly of Barnabas (1 Cor. 9:6; Gal. 2:1, 9, 13; Col. 4:10). (See also "The Missionary Church," p. 56.)

Barsabbas (bar-SAB-us) is the name of two different men in the New Testament. It is the surname of a man named Joseph who, along with Matthias, was nominated as an apostle to succeed Judas (Acts 1:23).

Barsabbas is also the surname of a man named Judas, a prophet of the Jerusalem church, who was sent with Silas to visit the church at Antioch and report the decisions of the Jerusalem council (Acts 15:22).

Bartholomew (bar-THOL-oh-mew) is one of the twelve apostles of Jesus who is mentioned in three of the gospels and Acts (Matt. 10:3; Mark 3:18; Luke 6:14; Acts 1:13) but not elsewhere in the New Testament.

Bartimeus (BAR-ti-MEE-us) is the name of a blind man whom Jesus healed as he went out from Jericho on the way to Jerusalem. His name is given only in Mark 10:46, but it is thought that this event is also found in the other synoptic gospels (Matt. 20:29-34; Luke 18:35-43).

Bashan (BAY-shan) was a broad plain located east of the Sea of Galilee. It was on the plains of Bashan that the Israelites defeated the Amorites in battle (Deut. 3:1-4).

Bathsheba (bath-SHEE-bah) was the wife of a man named Uriah, a soldier in the army of David. David fell in love with Bathsheba while Uriah was away in the army. David sent orders having Uriah placed in the front lines, where he was soon killed (2 Sam. 11). David then married Bathsheba, and she became the mother of four of his sons (2 Sam. 5:14; 1 Chron. 3:5). Solomon was the greatest and later a king of Israel and one of the ancestors of Jesus Christ (Matt. 1:6).

beatitude (bee-AT-ih-tyood), which means "blessedness," is a word not found in the English Bible. It may refer to the declarations of the joys of heaven or the blessings of God. Beatitudes occur quite often in the Old Testament (Ps. 32:1-2; 41:1). The gospels also contain isolated beatitudes, but the word is generally applied to those found in Matthew 5:3-11 and Luke 6:20-22, in which Jesus sets forth the qualities of disciples.

Beelzebub (bee-EL-zee-bub) is a name for Satan (see SATAN; and BAAL).

Belial (BEE-lee-al) is not used as a name in the Old Testament but is simply a word which means "worthless" or "wicked." Later, however, it is used as a name for evil and may be used as another name for Satan (see SATAN).

Belshazzar (bel-SHAZ-ar) was a grandson of Nebuchadnezzar and a king of Babylon. Daniel told him that God was displeased with him, and soon afterward Belshazzar was killed in battle (Dan. 5:1-30).

Benjamin (BEN-jah-min) was the youngest son of Jacob, and his mother was Rachel. She called him Benoni ("son of my sorrow") and died in bearing him (Gen. 35:18). Benjamin is also the name of one of the tribes of Israel (Josh. 18:21).

Beroea (ber-EE-uh) was a city of Macedonia (see maps F, G) where Paul founded a church on his second missionary journey (Acts 17:10-14). The Christians there were commended for their willingness to study scripture (Acts 17:11).

Bethel (BETH-el) is a town twelve miles north of Jerusalem (see maps A, B, C, E). The name means "house of God," and it was so named by Jacob after he met God there (Gen. 28:10-22).

Bethlehem (BETH-le-hem) is a town five miles from Jerusalem (see maps A,B,C,E). It was the burial place of Rachel (Gen. 35:16, 19), the home of Boaz (Ruth 2:1, 4). David was anointed there (1 Sam. 16:1, 13), and it was therefore called the "city of David" (Luke 2:4, 11). Its greatest importance for the Christian faith comes from the fact that Jesus was born there (Matt. 2:1; Luke 2:15-18).

Bible (BYE-b'l) is the name, originally meaning just "book," given to the collection of books which Christians regard as the inspired word of God. (See "The Authority of Scripture," p. 64.)

birthright (BIRTH-rite) was the special claim of the firstborn son among the Israelites. One right it included was a double portion of the inheritance of the family (Deut. 21:15-17). Esau lost his birthright to Jacob when he sold it for a meal (Gen. 25:27-34). Reuben lost his because of sin. His next brothers, Simeon and Levi, lost it because of violence; so their birthright came down to Judah (Gen. 49:3-10).

bishop (BISH-op) (See ELDERS.)

blasphemy (BLAS-feh-mee) means criticism or accusation of anyone. Usually it is thought of in regard to speaking lightly about God or about ideas or objects which should be spoken of reverently. In ancient Israel, blasphemy was punished by death (Lev. 24:10-16).

blessing (BLES-ing) is the bestowing of goodness by God (Gen. 1:22; 28; Ps. 1:1-3, etc.). When men bless God in return, they worship and praise him (Ps. 103:1-2). Sometimes men in the Bible give blessings to other men (Matt. 5:44, KJV; 1 Pet. 3:9). Finally, we can bless things by putting them aside for a special use (1 Cor. 10:16).

Boaz (BO-az) was a wealthy man of Bethlehem in the early days of Israel's judges. He married Ruth, a widow from Moab who had been the wife of one of his kinsmen (Ruth 2–4).

brazen serpent (BRAY-zen SER-pent) a snake or serpent made by Moses, and placed high on a pole. All those who looked at it were cured of the ailments caused when God sent fiery serpents among them because of their wickedness. Later, some of them mistakenly tried to worship it (Num. 21:4-9; 2 Kings 18:4).

bread was not only a common food in Bible times but a symbol of the life-giving quality of God (Gen. 3:19; Matt. 6:11). When baked without yeast, it has special meaning for both the Jewish and the Christian religions. This is the "unleavened bread" of the Jewish Passover (Exod.

12:15-20) and the Christian Communion or Lord's Supper (Matt. 26:26-28; 1 Cor. 11:23-26).

Jesus is also known as the "bread of life" (John 6:35, 48), meaning the one who truly gives life to men.

C

Caesar (SEE-zer) was the name of a famous Roman family. The name came to be used as the title of the Roman emperors. Augustus Caesar was the ruler when Jesus was born. The term occurs in the New Testament in Luke 20:22-25.

Caesarea (SES-uh-REE-uh) was a city built by the Jewish ruler Herod about twenty years before the birth of Jesus. It was named in honor of the Roman ruler under whom Herod served, Augustus Caesar. The city was located on the coast of the Mediterranean Sea about twenty-five miles northwest of Samaria (see map E). Caesarea was the home of Cornelius, to whom Peter preached (Acts 10). Philip the evangelist also lived in Caesarea (Acts 8:40; 21:8).

Caesarea Philippi (SES-uh-REE-uh FIL-ip-eye) was a town in northern Palestine about thirty miles inland from the coastal city of Tyre (see map E). It was a gift of the Roman emperor to the Jewish ruler, King Herod, who built a pagan temple there in honor of the emperor. The town was named Caesarea Philippi in order to distinguish it from the other Caesarea. The gospels report that Jesus was near Caesarea Philippi when he told his disciples about his coming suffering, death, and resurrection (Mark 8:27-33).

Caiaphas (KAY-uh-fus) was high priest from A.D. 18-36. He was the son-in-law of Annas, who had held that position before. Jesus was taken before Annas and then Caiaphas on the night of his arrest (John 18:12-28). But since the Jews could not legally execute him, he was then taken before Pilate. Caiaphas had earlier stated his belief that it would be a good idea for Jesus to die (John 11:41-53).

Cain (CANE) was the first son of Adam and Eve. He is generally remembered for murdering his brother, Abel, out of jealousy. Cain was also the father of a nation of people called Kenites. Also, Cain is the name of a village in Judah (Josh. 15:57, KJV).

calf worship was a part of ancient pagan religions. After God had delivered his people from captivity in Egypt, they made themselves a golden calf to worship while Moses was out of the camp (Exod. 32:4).

Calvary (KAL-vuh-ree), a Latin word meaning "skull," is the name of the place outside the walls of the city of Jerusalem where Jesus was crucified (Luke 23:33, KJV). It is also called Golgotha, which is the Hebrew word for "skull." The name was probably given the hill because it resembled the shape of a skull.

Cana (KAY-nah) was a city in the highlands of Galilee (see map E) where Jesus sometimes traveled during his ministry (John 2:1-11; 4:46-54; 21:2).

Canaan (KAY-nan) was an old name for the land of Palestine, the Israelites' promised land (see "The Exodus," p. 34).

Canaanites (KAY-nan-ites): the inhabitants of the land of Canaan (see maps A, B) when the Israelites came to possess it. The Israelites never completely drove them from the land.

Capernaum (kah-PUR-nay-um) was a village on the northwest shore of the Sea of Galilee (see map E). It was Jesus' headquarters during his Galilean ministry (Matt. 4:13; Mark 2:1). Though Jesus did a great deal of teaching and performed many miracles there, the people did not believe. He then predicted the destruction of the town (Luke 10:15), and his prophecy has come true.

captivity (kap-TIV-i-tee) in the Bible usually refers to the conquering of the kingdoms of Israel and Judah and the carrying off of their inhabitants as captives. This followed a series of invasions on the two nations who were weakened by sin and corruption. The Northern Kingdom, Israel, was finally taken captive by the Assyrians in 721 B.C. and the Southern Kingdom, Judah, by the Babylonians in 586 B.C. (see also "Kingdom and Exile," p. 36.)

Carmel (KAR-mel) is a mountain on the Mediterranean shore, west of the Sea of Galilee (see maps A,B,C,E). It was on Mount Carmel that Elijah won a contest against hundreds of pagan priests (1 Kings 18).

centurion (sen-TYOO-ri-un): a commander of a hundred soldiers in the army of the Roman Empire. Cornelius, the first Gentile to whom Peter preached, was a centurion (Acts 10).

Cephas (SEE-fas) means "rock" or "stone" and was the name given to the apostle Peter by Jesus (John 1:42).

Chaldea (kal-DEE-uh) is one name for the country which carried the Hebrew people of Judah off into captivity. Another name is Babylon or Babylonia.

chastisement (chas-TIZE-ment) means discipline or punishment. As a parent chastises his children, God also disciplines those he loves (Heb. 12:7-11).

children of God is a term which may refer to the nation of Israel (Exod. 4:22), to individual Israelites (Hos. 1:10), or to those whom God has redeemed from sin (John 1:12).

Children of Israel (See ISRAEL.)

Chloe (KLOH-ee) was a woman of the Corinthian church whom Paul knew (1 Cor. 1:11).

Christ (See "Lord and Christ," p. 49; and "Christ," p. 90.)

Christian (KRIS-chun) is a word, occurring only three times in the New Testament, used to describe followers of Christ. It was first used in Antioch by non-Christians (Acts 11:26). It became a name for which followers of Jesus suffered in times of persecution (1 Pet. 4:16).

Chronicles, 1 and 2 (See "History," pp. 13-14.)

church (See ch. 6.)

circumcision (SIR-kum-SIH-zhun) was a sign of the covenant between God and the Hebrew people. It involved a cutting away of the foreskin on all male Israelites (Gen. 17:10; Lev. 12:3).

Colossians (See "Letters," p. 23-25.)

commandments (kuh-MAND-ments) are laws, directions, or guidelines for life. The Ten Commandments were given to Moses at Mount Sinai. They are (1) have no other gods, (2) do not make or worship idols, (3) do not speak God's name in a trite or vain way, (4)

honor the Sabbath, (5) honor your father and mother, (6) do not kill, (7) do not commit adultery, (8) do not steal, (9) do not falsely witness or lie about anyone, (10) do not covet or want things which belong to others. These laws were given by God to his people after he led them safely out of Egyptian slavery, in order to protect and help them.

communion (kuh-MEWN-yun) is a word for coming together and sharing in fellowship. It is a name sometimes given to the Lord's Supper (see "Lord's Supper," p. 94).

community (kuh-MEW-ni-tee) means a group of people who share some sort of bond. Christians form a community in the church (see "The Church as a New Community," p. 52).

concubine (KON-kew-bine) is a name for an additional wife in the Old Testament days when men sometimes had several. A concubine did not have the same privileges and status as the first wife (Gen. 16; 21:10; Judges 8:31).

confession (kun-FES-shun) may refer to the acknowledgment of sin before God (1 John 1:9) or the acknowledgment of our faith in something, chiefly in the lordship of Christ (Rom. 10:9-10; Phil. 2:11).

consecration (kon-see-KRAY-shun) refers to the dedication of something or someone to a specific purpose (Exod. 13:2; Num. 3:12). In the Old Testament, the Levites were consecrated for the priesthood. Christians are consecrated as they devote their lives to the service and worship of God (Rom. 12:1-2).

conversion (kun-VER-zhun) means literally "a turning." It usually refers to a turning from sin to faith in God and Jesus Christ (see ch. 9).

Corinth (KOR-inth) is an ancient Greek city (see maps D,F,G) which was the capital of the province of Achaia in the Roman Empire. Paul preached and founded a church there (Acts 18:1; see also "The Missionary Church," p. 56).

Corinthians 1 and 2 (See "Letters," pp. 23-25.)

Cornelius (kor-NEEL-yus) was a Roman centurion converted by Peter (Acts 10; see also "The Universal Church," p. 54).

council (KOUN-s'l) in the New Testament refers to the Jewish Sanhedrin or other courts of law (Matt. 26:59; Mark 13:9; Acts 5:34) or to the Jerusalem council.

covenant (KUV-eh-nant) (See p. 91.)

creation (kree-AY-shun) (See pp. 29 and 92.)

Crete (KREET) is an island in the Mediterranean Sea (see maps D,F,G) where Paul and Titus established a church (Titus 1:5-14). The people who lived there were considered immoral and were not respected.

crucifixion (kroo-si-FIX-shun) (See p. 92.)

Cyprus (SIGH-prus) is an island in the eastern part of the Mediterranean Sea (see maps D,F,G). Paul preached and founded a church there (Acts 13:4-12).

D

Damascus (duh-MAS-kus) is an ancient city of Syria (see maps D,F,G). David once conquered this city (2 Sam. 8:5-6). Paul's conversion took place near Damascus (Acts 9:1-19).

Dan was the fifth son of Jacob and thus head of one of the twelve tribes of Israel (Gen. 30:6; see map B). The land allotted to this tribe was a fertile area but was troubled because the Philistines were so near.

Daniel (DAN-yuhl) was one of Israel's greatest prophets. He was taken from Jerusalem to Babylon by King Nebuchadnezzar in 605 B.C. (Dan. 1:1, 3, 6). Daniel is chiefly remembered because of his refusal to worship Babylon's false gods and because of the book of Daniel (see p. 17). Because of his faithfulness, God granted Daniel  the gift of interpreting dreams, and great wisdom (Dan. 1:17, 20; 2:13).

David (DAY-vid) was Israel's greatest king, and ruler for forty years. As a boy he killed the giant, Goliath (1 Sam. 17). Later he played the harp for King Saul and became a friend of Saul's son, Jonathan. It was King David who made Jerusalem the capital of Israel. The book of 1 Samuel tells the story of his great reign.

David was a man of great feeling; and though he committed some serious sins, he was deeply repentant. He wrote many of the Psalms, expressing a wide range of emotions, attitudes, and ideas. He was called a "man after God's own heart" (1 Sam. 13:14; Acts 13:22). (See also "Kingdom and Exile," p. 36.)

Day of Atonement (See ATONEMENT, DAY OF.)

Day of the Lord is a phrase which refers to the final display of God's power in the defeat of all evil. It is associated with the appearing of Christ and the final judgment of all people (Isa. 2:12-21; Luke 21:7-33; Rev. 21:1).

Day of Pentecost (See PENTECOST, DAY OF.)

deacon (DEE-kun) comes from a Greek word meaning "to serve." It is a word for men in the early church who were appointed to perform special tasks or services (Acts 6:1-8; 2 Cor. 8:4; 1 Tim. 3).

deaconess (DEE-kun-es) is the female form of the word "deacon" and also means "one who serves." Paul used this word in referring to Phoebe, a woman of the early church who had been of great help to him (Rom. 16:1-2).

Dead Sea: an inland sea in Palestine, sometimes called the Salt Sea (Gen. 14:3). It is forty-seven miles long and ten miles wide (see maps A-G). It is called the Dead Sea because the great amount of salt in it prevents anything from living in the water. It is four times as salty as the ocean. The Dead Sea is 1,300 feet below sea level and has no outlet. The Jordan River ends when it flows into the Dead Sea.

Dead Sea Scrolls (SKROHLZ) were discovered in 1947 in caves on the northwest shore of the Dead Sea near Qumran (see map E). The scrolls date from about the first century before Christ. They contain many fragments of the Old Testament and other writings of a small Jewish group called the Essenes. (See also "The Dead Sea Scrolls," p. 87.)

Deborah (DEB-oh-ruh) was the fourth judge of Israel and one of the greatest who ever served the nation (Judg. 4–5). Israel had been unable to unite for action as a nation since the conquest, 175 years before. But with Deborah's vision and inspiring presence, they overcame the Hazorites at Mount Tabor (see map A).

decalogue (DEK-uh-log) means literally "ten words" and is another name for the Ten Commandments.

Dedication, Feast of (DED-i-KAY-shun): a yearly Jewish celebration lasting for eight days to mark the time the Temple was restored between the Old and New Testaments. It is sometimes called the Feast of Lights. It was at this celebration that Jesus spoke in John 10:24-30.

Delilah (dee-LIE-luh) was a wicked Philistine woman who tricked the strong man Samson into losing the strength God had given him (Judg. 16:4-20).

Demas (DEE-mus) was a good friend and helper to Paul while he was in prison in Rome (Col. 4:14). Later he deserted Paul and went to Thessalonica (2 Tim. 4:10).

Demetrius (deh-MEE-tree-us) was a silversmith in Ephesus who made his living by making and selling silver images of the goddess Artemis. Because Paul's preaching in Ephesus was causing him to lose business, Demetrius raised a mob against him (Acts 19:23-27).

demons (DEE-munz) were evil spirits which during Jesus' day possessed people and caused such things as insanity and disease. The New Testament teaches that Jesus has authority and power over demons and protects his disciples from them (Matt. 12:22; Luke 8:26-36; Eph. 6:10-12).

Derbe (DUR-bee) was a city in Asia Minor visited several times by Paul (Acts 14:20; 16:1; see maps F, G).

Deuteronomy (See p. 13.)

devil (DEV-ul) is one of the many names for Satan, the enemy of both God and man.

diadem (DIE-uh-dem) is a symbol of complete power. It may be a special headpiece such as a king's crown or turban. Or it may be a staff which is held in the hand (Rev. 19:12).

Diana (die-AN-uh) (See ARTEMIS.)

diaspora (die-AS-por-ruh) means "a scattering," and refers to Jews who were taken to live outside of Palestine. By the time of Christ, there were many more Diaspora Jews than Jews living in Palestine.

Dinah (DIE-nah) was the daughter of Jacob and Leah (Gen. 30:21) and thus sister or half-sister to the founders of the twelve tribes of Israel.

disciple (dih-SIGH-p'l): one who follows a particular leader or teacher. The word is often applied to Jesus' twelve apostles in the gospels but more frequently it describes any Christian (Acts 6:1-2, 7; 9:36).

Dorcas (DOR-kus) (See TABITHA.)

dualism (DYOO-ul-izm) (See p. 30.)

E

earnest (ER-nest) is a sum of money or goods given when an agreement is made, to guarantee the complete payment or fulfillment of promises. The apostle Paul tells us that God sends his Spirit to Christians as an earnest or downpayment which guarantees that we may trust in him (2 Cor. 1:22; 5:5).

Ebal (EE-b'l) is a mountain in Samaria important in the history of Israel. Jacob's well was located at the foot of Mount Ebal and the city of Shechem was not far away (see maps A, B, C, E). Every year the people of Israel would recite the blessings and curses of the Law, with those standing on nearby Mount Gerizim giving the blessings and those on Mount Ebal the curses (Deut. 27:4-26).

Ecclesiastes (See p. 15.)

Eden (EE-d'n) is the name of the garden where Adam and Eve lived until they sinned and were sent out of it (Gen. 2–3).

Edomites (EE-dom-ites) were the nation of people descending from Esau (Gen. 25:30; 36:1, 8). The land of Edom was located south of the Dead Sea (see maps A, B, C). A great rivalry and conflict between the Jews and the Edomites lasted for many centuries (Ps. 137:7; Ezek. 25:12-14; Obad. 10-14).

Egypt (EE-jipt) is a country in northeast Africa (see maps D, F, G). In the Old Testament, it is important as the place where Israel suffered captivity from which Moses led them in the exodus. Later, Jesus' parents took him as a child to Egypt in order to escape wicked King Herod's efforts to find and kill him (Matt. 2:13-15).

Ehud (EE-hud) was an Israelite judge who led the Israelites against the Moabites in a battle in which he killed the king of Moab. Eighty years of peace followed, lasting until Ehud's death (Judg. 3:15-30).

elders (ELD-erz) was originally a term for older men in each community who are leaders. The New Testament tells us that such men guided the early churches. They were required to be blameless and true to the faith (1 Tim. 3:1-7;

Titus 1:5-9). In the early church, elders were also called bishops.

election (ee-LEK-shun) is a word used to describe both God's choosing of the nation of Israel as his people and his offering of salvation to all men through Jesus Christ (1 Pet. 2:9-10).

Eli (EE-lie) was a judge and high priest in ancient Israel. He was the priest to whom Hannah came when she prayed for a son. After the son (Samuel) was born, he lived with Eli in the tabernacle. Eli died when he broke his neck from a fall caused by the news that his sons had been killed and the ark of the covenant taken in battle (1 Sam. 1–4).

Elias (ee-LIE-us) is the Greek form of the name Elijah.

Elijah (ee-LIE-juh) was one of the greatest prophets of the Old Testament. One of the many things for which he is remembered is his contest with priests of the false god Baal on Mount Carmel (1 Kings 18:17-40). Elijah is one of the few men of the Bible who did not die but was taken by God (2 Kings 2:1-15). His successor was named Elisha.

Elisha (ee-LIE-shah) was a great prophet whose ministry was filled with miracles. He was anointed by Elijah to be his successor. He is remembered for finally destroying Baal worship. Also, he healed the Syrian, Naaman, from leprosy (2 Kings 5).

Elizabeth (ee-LIZ-uh-beth) or Elisabeth was the wife of Zechariah the priest. When she was old she had a son who became known as John the Baptist (Luke 1:5-66).

Elohim (eh-LO-him) is the most frequent Hebrew name for God. It is used over 2,500 times in the Old Testament.

El Shaddai (el SHAD-uh-eye), which probably means "almighty God," is the name by which God was known to Abraham, Isaac, and Jacob (Exod. 6:3).

Elymas (EL-ih-mus) was a magician on the island of Cyprus on whom Paul placed a curse on his first missionary journey (Acts 13:4-12).

embalm (em-BALM or em-BAHM) is a word for an ancient Egyptian process of using oil and spices in preparing a body for burial. Both Jacob and Joseph were embalmed (Gen. 50:2-3, 26).

Emmanuel (eh-MAN-you-el) (See IMMANUEL.)

Enoch (EE-nuhk) was a man of God who is remembered for his great faith. The Old Testament says that Enoch "walked with God" and did not die (Gen. 5:24; Heb. 11:2, 5).

Epaphras (EP-uh-frus) was one of Paul's helpers who may have founded the church at Colossae (see maps F, G). Paul calls him a "fellow prisoner," so some have thought that Epaphras was in prison with Paul (Col. 1:7).

Epaphroditus (ee-PAF-roh-DIE-tus) was a messenger sent by the Philippian church with gifts to Paul while he was imprisoned in Rome (Phil. 2:25; 4:18).

Ephesians (See p. 25.)

Ephesus (EF-eh-sus) was the capital city of the Roman state of Asia (see maps F, G). It was a very old city at the mouth of the river Cayster. Ephesus was important because it was on the road from Rome to places in the eastern part of the empire. It was also an important shipping center with a good harbor.

The apostle Paul worked in Ephesus for over two years and from the city directed other missionaries in inland towns. Years after Paul lived there, the apostle John lived in Ephesus. (See also "The Missionary Church," p. 56.)

ephod (EF-ud) is the name of a special vest worn by the Jewish high priest. It was brightly colored (gold, blue, purple, and scarlet) and had twelve precious stones attached to it with gold chains. These stones represented the twelve tribes of Israel. In later years, persons other than the high priest wore ephods (1 Sam. 2:18; 2 Sam. 6:14).

Ephraim (EE-freh-im) was the youngest of Joseph's two sons. Ephraim and his brother Manasseh were fathers of two of the twelve tribes of Israel (see map B). These two tribes fought with each other for some time. The land which the tribe of Ephraim inhabited was much better than that of Manasseh.

Esau (EE-saw) was the son of Isaac and Rebecca and the older twin of Jacob. He sold his birthright to Jacob one day when he was very hungry and later tried to kill Jacob for tricking him out of their father's blessing (Gen. 25:30-34; 27). Later, however, he and Jacob were reconciled (Gen. 32:6–33:16).

epistle (ee-PIS'l) means a letter. Twenty-one of the books of the New Testament are actually letters written to different individuals and churches by God-directed men (see "Letters," p. 23; and "The Writings of the Church," p. 59).

eschatology (es-kuh-TOL-oh-jee) is the study of the "last things" often mentioned in the Bible. These include death, the resurrection, the second coming of Christ, end of the age, judgment, etc.

Essenes (eh-SEENZ) is the name of one of the many groups of Jews existing in the time of Christ. Among other groups were those called Pharisees, Sadducees, and Zealots. The Essenes were strict and lived apart from other Jews. The Dead Sea Scrolls were apparently preserved and used by a group of Essenes living on the desert near the Dead Sea. (See also "The Dead Sea Scrolls," p. 87.)

Esther (ES-ter) was a Jewish orphan girl who became queen of Persia. As queen, she saved the Jewish people from destruction by the king. The book of Esther in the Old Testament recounts the story of Esther, and each year the Feast of Purim honors her.

eternal life (ee-TER-nuhl) is the type of life promised to those who accept Jesus Christ in faith and are obedient to him. It means more than just life that does not end; it is an altogether different kind of life, like that which God revealed in Jesus (1 John 5:11-12). Eternal life begins when we become disciples of Jesus Christ, experiencing a new birth (John 3; Gal. 2:20; Titus 3:4-7).

eternity (ee-TER-ni-tee) is the name for time that has no beginning or ending point. It is also one of the qualities of God (Jer. 1:5; Ps. 90).

Ethiopia (EE-thee-OH-pe-uh) is an African country just south of Egypt. Cush, the grandson of Noah, went to live in this area (Gen. 10:6-8).

eunuch (YOU-nuhk) is a term for a type of male servant or officer in some royal courts. The man to whom Philip the evangelist preached in Acts 8 was a eunuch, a treasurer of the queen, from Ethiopia.

Euphrates (you-FRAY-teez) is a great river of western Asia (see map D), one of the four near which the garden of Eden was located (Gen. 2:14). In the Old Testament, it is frequently called "the great river" or just "the river" (Gen. 15:18; Deut. 1:7; Isa. 8:7).

Eutychus (YOU-tih-kus) was a boy in Troas who went to sleep and fell out a window while Paul was preaching. He was killed by the fall, but the apostle restored his life (Acts 20:7-12). His name means "lucky."

evangelist (ee-VAN-juh-list) means one who announces good news, or one who tells the gospel of Jesus Christ. The New Testament gives examples of apostles, elders, deacons, and others serving as evangelists (Acts 8:25; Acts 21:8; 1 Cor. 1:17; 2 Tim. 4:2-5).

Eve was the first woman, created by God as a suitable companion for Adam (Gen. 2:20-24). Her name means "mother of all living."

exile (EKS-ile) when used in reference to the Old Testament usually means the period of time when Israel was held captive by Assyria or when Judah was held in Babylon (see "Kingdom and Exile," p. 36).

exodus (EKS-oh-dus) means "a going out" and generally refers to God's miraculous leading of Israel out of Egyptian captivity (see p. 34). The exodus begins with God's calling of Moses and ends with the giving of the Law to Israel at Mount Sinai. The exodus is remembered because of the way it shows God's power and his love for his people. The story of the exodus is told in the Old Testament book titled Exodus (see p. 12).

exorcism (EK-sor-sizm) is a term for the practice of expelling demons through the use of supposed magic, charms, spells, or, in New Testament times, by the power of Christ. Acts 19:13-16 tells of some Jewish exorcists who tried to use Jesus' name as a magical power to cast out demons.

Ezekiel (ee-ZEE-kee-el) was a Hebrew prophet during the time when Judah was exiled in Babylon. His work lasted from about 593-571 B.C. He was a powerful preacher and also used symbols to communicate God's word. The book of Ezekiel in the Old Testament contains his writings (see p. 17).

Ezra (EZ-ruh) (See p. 15.)

F

faith (See "The Call of Abraham," p. 32, and "Faith," p. 92.)

fall of man, the: an expression used to refer to man's turning away from God and the entrance of sin into the world. Adam and Eve's sin, or fall, brought death into the world. Since their first sin, all men eventually come into contact with sin (Rom. 3:10-26; 5:12).

famine (FAM-in) means a time when food supply is very short.

Famines occurred rather often in ancient Egypt and Palestine, since rainfall was scarce in some years and crops were sometimes destroyed by pests such as locusts and caterpillars. War could cut off food supplies as well. One of the worst of the biblical famines is that told of in Genesis 41, when Joseph's brothers came to Egypt for food, only to find that the brother they had sold into slavery was now ruling Egypt.

fasting (FAST-ing) means doing without food. In Israel, there was a period of fasting before some of the religious feasts. Often people would fast on special occasions or before a period of prayer. The Bible tells us that Jesus fasted for forty days in the wilderness at the beginning of his ministry (Matt. 4:2). But he also criticized those who fasted only to be seen by others (Matt. 6:16).

feasts were sacred celebrations in Israel which were occasions of public worship. There were seven special feasts: Passover, Pentecost, Trumpets, Atonement, Tabernacles or Booths, Lights or Dedication, and Purim. These feasts mostly celebrated special events in Israel's history and called Israel to thank God for his care and blessings.

fellowship (FEL-oh-ship) comes from a word meaning "to share" or "to have in common." Christians who share their faith in Christ also share their time and money with one another (Acts 2:44-46; see also "The Church as a New Community," p. 52). Christians are in fellowship with each other.

firstborn refers to an oldest child or animal (Exod. 11:5). The firstborn children were important in Israel because the men received a double portion of the family inheritance and became head of the household. Firstborn animals were sacrificed as offerings to God (Exod. 13:13, 15; 34:20). Because of his resurrection, Jesus is called the "firstborn from the dead" (Col. 1:18).

first fruits refers to the earliest products of fields, orchards, and herds each year. They were seen as an assurance of the coming harvest. They were also used in supporting the priesthood, who did not cultivate their own crops, and in special offerings (Exod. 23:19; Lev. 23:10, 17; Deut. 26:1-11).

flood when used in the Bible usually tells of a great, year-long flood with which God destroyed much that was on the earth because of its sinfulness. Noah and his family were saved, and from them all men descend (Gen. 6–8).

forerunner (FORE-run-er) means one who goes before and prepares the way. John the Baptist was Jesus' forerunner (Luke 3:4, 6).

forgiveness (for-GIV-nes) (See "Baptism," p. 89.)

fornication (FOR-ni-KAY-shun) refers to sexual acts between two persons who are not married to each other. It is condemned in the New Testament (Matt. 15:19; 1 Cor. 6:9, 18) and the Old Testament, where it was sometimes involved in heathen worship (Jer. 2:20; 3:6).

frankincense (FRANK-in-sens) is a perfume made from balsam trees. Frankincense was among the gifts the wise men brought to the infant Jesus (Matt. 2:11-12).

freeman is a slave who has been given his freedom. On one occasion, however, Paul uses the term when he is talking about people receiving spiritual freedom from sin (1 Cor. 7:22).

G

Gabriel (GAY-bree-el), which means "man of God," is the name of an angel mentioned four times in the Bible (Dan. 8:16; 9:21; Luke 1:11-20, 26-35).

Gad was Jacob's seventh son and the head of one of the twelve tribes of Israel (Josh. 20:8; see map B).

Galatia (guh-LAY-shah) was a province of the Roman Empire in Asia Minor (see maps F, G) where Paul traveled a great deal. One of his letters was written to the churches of this area.

Galatians (See p. 25.)

Galilean (GAL-ih-LEE-un) means one who was born in or lived in Galilee.

Galilee (GAL-ih-lee) was one of the three provinces of Palestine in Jesus' day (see map E). Jesus grew up in Galilee and preached his first sermon in the synagogue at Nazareth. His disciples were also all Galileans, and it was in Galilee that Jesus performed his first miracle (John 2:11).

Galilee, Sea of: a small inland sea sixty miles north of Jerusalem and to the east of the province of Galilee (see maps A, B, C, E). In the New Testament it is also called the "Lake of Gennesaret" (Luke 5:1) and the "Sea of Tiberias"

(John 6:1; 21:1). Its ancient name was the "Sea of Chinnereth" (Num. 34:11; Josh. 13:27). It is thirteen miles long and eight miles wide.

Gallio (GAL-ee-oh) was a Roman official known for his good attitude. Paul was brought before Gallio, but the official refused to hear any charges against the apostle (Acts 18:12-17).

Gamaliel (guh-MAY-lee-el) was a Jewish leader who urged other Jewish leaders not to kill the apostles (Acts 5:34-40). He was also one of Paul's teachers before Paul was a Christian (Acts 22:3).

Garden of Eden (See EDEN.)

Garden of Gethsemane (See GETHSEMANE.)

Gehazi (gee-HAY-zie) was a servant of the prophet Elisha. He is remembered for having lied to receive payment from Naaman, a leper Elisha had cured. Because of this, Gehazi was punished by receiving Naaman's leprosy (2 Kings 5:1-27).

genealogy (JEN-ee-AL-oh-jee) is a list of the generations of a family, usually traced through fathers and sons. Matthew begins his gospel by giving a genealogy of Jesus (Matt. 1:1-17), and Luke gives an even fuller one (Luke 3:23-38). Genealogies were important to Israel for a number of reasons, such as determining family inheritances.

General Epistles (See "Letters," p. 23.)

Genesis (See p. 12.)

Gennesaret (geh-NES-uh-ret) is a flat area of land on the northwest shore of the Sea of Galilee. It is also a name by which the Sea of Galilee itself is sometimes called (Luke 5:1).

Gentiles (JEN-tilez) are those people who are not of Jewish origin. In the time of Christ, the Jews considered all Gentiles their enemies, but Jesus brought good news of God's love for all men, Gentiles included (Rom. 3:29-30; see also "The Universal Church," p. 54).

Gerizim (geh-RYE-zim) is a mountain in Samaria, very near Mount Ebal (see maps A, B, C, E). When the Israelites returned from exile in Babylon, they refused to let the Samaritans, who had mixed with other races, rebuild Jerusalem. So the Samaritans built themselves another temple on Mt. Gerizim (Ezra 4:1-4; Neh. 2:19-20). It was about this temple that the Samaritan woman asked Jesus (John 4:19-21).

Gethsemane (geth-SEM-uh-nee) was the name of a garden on the Mount of Olives near Jerusalem, where Jesus prayed and was arrested on the night before his crucifixion (Mark 14:32-50).

giants (JIE-ants) are frequently mentioned in the Old Testament, sometimes meaning simply "warriors" or "mighty men" (Job 16:14, KJV). But sometimes the Hebrew word does mean very tall, powerful men (Deut. 2:11, 20, KJV). Goliath is the best-known giant of the Old Testament, and he may have been nine feet tall or more (1 Sam. 17).

Gideon (GID-ee-un) was one of Israel's great judges (see Judg. 6–8). He is especially remembered for his great faith in defeating a large army of Midianites with an army of only 300 men. Gideon was also named Jerubbaal (Judg. 6:28-32).

Gilead (GIL-ee-ad) was the name for the land of Israel east of the Jordan River from the lower end of the Sea of Galilee to the top of the Dead Sea (see maps B, C, E). Jacob camped there when running from Laban (Gen. 31:7-43).

Gilgal (GIL-gal) is located about ten miles from the Jordan River near Jericho (see maps A,B,C). It was the site of the first camp made by the Israelites after crossing the Jordan River (Josh. 4:19-20).

God is never actually defined in the Bible, though his presence fills it. We can learn many things about what God is like from reading both the Old and New Testaments. For example, we know that he is not limited by space as we are but is present everywhere at the same time (Ps. 139). We know that his wisdom is greater than any earthly wisdom (Job 28; Prov. 8:1, 22-31). He is holy in a way that sets him completely apart from all men (Lev. 19:2). He is kind and loving above all that we can achieve or even imagine (Exod. 34:6-7; Ps. 86; 103; 145). The wrath or anger that he sometimes expresses is a result of his love for mankind and concern for their welfare (Num. 25:11; Deut. 6:15; Isa. 54:7-8). He is the one and only creator and sustainer of all that is (Exod. 20:3; 1 Kings 18:17-46; Isa. 2:8, 18). But we learn the most about God from the life and teachings of Jesus (Heb. 1:1-4), since "God was in Christ" (2 Cor. 5:19). We learn that he desires a close relationship with his creatures, as father to son or daughter (Mark 14:36; Rom. 8:15; Gal. 4:6). We learn that the wrath he feels toward sin actually involves suffering on his part because of the greatness of his love, which cannot ignore sin (Rom. 11:22). We learn that he desires us to be like him (2 Pet. 1:4) and that we can come closer to him in Jesus Christ than was ever before possible (Rom. 8:15-17; 1 John 4:15-16).

godhead refers to the quality of being divine. It means *godhood* very much like *manhood* means the quality of being a man. While the King James Version prefers this word, the Revised Standard Version often uses the word "deity" (Acts 17:29; Col. 2:9).

godliness (GOD-lee-nes) describes a way of thinking and acting that is obedient to God and kind and loving to other people (1 Tim. 4:7-8).

Golgotha (GOL-go-thuh) (See CALVARY.)

Goliath (go-LIE-ath) was a giant Philistine soldier. He was probably over nine feet tall and possibly as much as eleven. He was defeated by the youth David, who was armed only with a sling and five stones (1 Sam. 17).

Gomorrah (go-MOR-uh) was an evil city destroyed by God in the days of Abraham (Gen. 13:10; 19:24). Though its exact location is not known, it was somewhere near the south end of the Dead Sea, near Zoar (see map A).

gopher wood (GO-fer) was the kind of wood out of which Noah built the ark (Gen. 6:14).

gospel (GOS-pel) means "good news." It refers to the message of what God has done for men in the life, death, and resurrection of Jesus of Nazareth.

gospels (See p. 21.)

grace (See p. 93.)

graven image (GRAY-ven IM-aj): an idol carved from wood, stone, or metal (Isa. 40:20; 44:16-17).

great commission (kuh-MISH-un): the important charge Jesus gave his followers, before his ascension, to take the gospel to all the world (Matt. 28:19-20).

Greece is a once-powerful nation located in southeast Europe (see maps F,G). Paul visited several Grecian cities on his missionary journeys (Acts 16:11–18:18; 20:1-6). Residents of Greece or those who spoke Greek were called Grecians.

Greek is a term sometimes used in the New Testament to describe not only those who live in Greece but any non-Jews or foreigners as well (Rom. 1:16).

    Greek is also a language that was very influential in the time of Jesus and in which most of the New Testament is written (see "Languages of the Bible," p. 4).

guilt (GILT) (See p. 77.)

H

Habakkuk (See. p. 18.)

Hades (HAY-deez) is the place of the dead, also called Sheol (Acts 2:27; Rev. 1:18; 6:8).

Hagar (HAY-gar) was an Egyptian maidservant of Sarah, Abraham's wife. Sarah gave Hagar to Abraham for a second wife and she had a son, Ishmael (Gen. 16).

Haggai (See p. 19.)

hallelujah (HAL-eh-LOO-yah) is a Hebrew term used in worship. It means "Praise Jehovah" or "Praise you the Lord" (Pss. 106, 111–113).

Ham was Noah's youngest son and became the father of many nations (Gen. 10:6-20).

Haman (HAY-man) was an enemy of the Jews in the days of Esther. He died on the gallows which he had made for a leading Jew, Mordecai (Esth. 7).

handmaid: a female slave or servant. Sometimes women who were not servants would also use the term when speaking of themselves, showing humility (Ruth 3:9; 1 Sam. 1:11; Luke 1:38).

Hannah (HAN-uh) was the wife of Elkanah and mother of Samuel, the great prophet and last of Israel's judges. For many years, Hannah had no children. She promised that if God would let her have a son she would give him to God as his servant. The son she dedicated to the Lord was Samuel (1 Sam. 1).

Haran (HAY-ran) was the city of Abraham's early life from which he set out for Canaan (Gen. 12:4; see map D).

heart, in the Bible, means far more than just the organ which pumps blood through the body. It might refer to the intellect or imagination (Gen. 6:5), the feelings (Gen. 18:5, KJV), or the will (Ps. 119:2). Sometimes it also means a person's affections, much as we use the word today (Ps. 62:10). Or the heart may sometimes mean one's whole nature (Gen. 6:6; Jer. 17:9).

heathen (HEE-th'n) is generally used in the Bible to mean the same as Gentiles, or non-Israelites.

heaven (HEV-'n) is a name for the dwelling place of God (Ps. 11:4), sometimes thought of as "beyond the sky." Of course it is important to know also that God is with us at all times. The Bible does not say "where" heaven is, or answer all our other questions about it. The Bible does assure us that after we die we will be resurrected to be with God in heaven (Matt. 5:12; 6:20; Eph. 3:15).

Hebrew (HEE-broo) is a name for a descendant of Abraham, a member of the nation of Israel. It may come from a word meaning "to cross over the river." Hebrew is also the name of the language spoken by these people (see "Languages of the Bible," p. 4).

Hebrews: a New Testament book (See p. 26).

Hebron (HEE-brun) is one of the world's oldest cities. It was an early camping place for Abraham (Gen. 13:18), nineteen miles southwest of Jerusalem (see maps A, B, C, E).

hell is the name of a place and the condition of men who have turned away from God. It is a place of torment and darkness (Matt. 8:12; Rev. 14:10). In the King James Version, it also refers to Hades, the place of the dead.

Hellenists (HEL-en-ists) in the New Testament were Jews who had adopted Greek customs and speech (Acts 6:1; 9:29).

heresy (HEH-re-see) is a false teaching about God or his will for men. Those following and teaching such false ideas are called "heretics" (2 Pet. 2:1).

Herod (HEH-rud) is the name of a line of rulers of Palestine from 47 B.C. to A.D. 79. Herod the Great was called king of the Jews from 37 until 4 B.C. It was he who killed all the baby boys in Bethlehem when he heard that a new king had been born there (Matt. 2:1-18). His three sons divided the kingdom after his death. One of them ordered John the Baptist killed (Matt. 14:1-12). His grandson was Herod Agrippa.

Herodias (heh-RO-dee-us) was the wicked granddaughter of Herod the Great who played a role in the killing of John the Baptist (Matt. 14:3-12; Mark 6:14-29; Luke 3:19-20).

Hezekiah (HEZ-eh-KIE-uh) was king of Judah for twenty-nine years (724–695 B.C.). He cleansed the Temple and tried to restore proper worship to God in evil times (2 Kings 18–20; 2 Chron. 29–32).

Hiram (HIGH-r'm) was king of Tyre and a friend of both David and Solomon. He supplied builders and materials for both kings (2 Sam. 5:11; 1 Kings 5:1).

history is the story of the past. Many books of the Bible record history (see pp. 13 and 23).

Hittites (HIT-ites) were a people who were one of the greatest threats to early Israel (see map A). From the time of Abraham, they lived among the Israelites, especially in the central hills (Num. 13:29; Josh. 11:3), often intermarrying with the Jewish people. By the time of Solomon, the Hittites were in the position of servants (1 Kings 9:20).

holiness (HOLE-ee-nes) comes from a Hebrew word meaning separateness or withdrawal. In the Bible it is mainly applied to God (Exod. 3:5; 15:11; Isa. 52:10; Jer. 23:9). The New Testament teaches the holiness of Jesus Christ as well (Mark 1:24; Luke 4:34; Rev. 3:7). Because of Christ's death and resurrection, the church can also be holy, or "sanctified" (1 Cor. 1:2; 6:11; Eph. 2:19). The Christian's life is also to be holy (Rom. 12:1), which means righteous and pure in a way which can only be through Jesus Christ.

Holy of holies, also called the "most holy place," was a division of the tabernacle (Israel's portable place of worship) and later of the Temple. It was separated from another division, the "holy place," by a heavy veil. In it was the ark of the covenant. It could be entered only by the high priest, and only at certain times (Heb. 9:1-7).

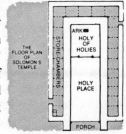

Holy Ghost, Holy Spirit: the divine creative force at the beginning of the world (Gen. 1:2), who also inspired the Bible writers (John 16:13), and who lives in Christians (Acts 5:32). The King James word "ghost" meant "spirit." (See "The Inspiration of Scripture," p. 65; and "Holy Spirit," p. 94.)

hope is desiring God's future blessing and expecting to receive it. It is an important difference between the Christian and the non-Christian. Hope includes trust in God in times when all seems lost. It is based on faith that God will love, protect, and care for those who turn to him (Rom. 15:13; 2 Cor. 3:12; 2 Thess. 2:16).

Horeb (HO-reb) was the mountain where God called Moses. Centuries later the prophet Elijah fled to Mount Horeb when evil men were seeking to take his life (1 Kings 19:8). This mountain is sometimes identified with Mount Sinai, but its exact location is uncertain.

hosannah (ho-ZAN-uh) was an exclamation shouted in Hebrew worship. It means "save now" or "praise to the highest." The people waved palm leaves and shouted "Hosanna" as Jesus rode into Jerusalem on his last entry (Matt. 21:9).

Hosea (See p. 17.)

humility (hyoo-MIL-i-tee) means freedom from selfishness in every way. Humility grows out of knowing God's love and the strength God gives us to help and be kind to others. There is a false humility which seeks to appear humble but only to draw attention from others (Col. 2:18, 23).

hypocrisy (hih-POK-rih-see) means pretending to be something that one is not. A hypocrite is not a person who tries to do good but makes mistakes. A hypocrite is a person who really does not try to do good—he only wants to appear to be doing so. Jesus was very critical of these people who "play-acted" their religion (Matt. 6:1-18; 23:13-36).

I

idol (EYE-d'l) means a false god, whether it be one made of wood, stone, or some other material, or one that is really some part of our lives that should not be so important to us (see "Why Some Christians Drift Away from Christ," p. 80).

idolatry (eye-DOL-uh-tree) is the worship of false gods or idols. Israel's neighboring countries were idolatrous, worshiping such things as the sun and moon, trees, mountains and springs, and even things they had made by hand (Judg. 6:25-32). God's chosen people were themselves often idolatrous. Immediately after God had led them out of Egyptian captivity,  they built and worshiped a golden calf (Exod. 32:4). People today are more often idolatrous not by worshiping things such as mountains, but by placing other things between themselves and God. For example, they may be more interested in money or clothes than they are in obeying God.

image of God (IM-aj): the way in which man was created something like God (Gen. 1:26-27). This does not mean that God looks like man. It means that man has a spirit and is able to communicate with and love others. Since sin entered the world through man, life is like a broken mirror—we can still see the image, faintly, but sin has damaged the image of God in man. Jesus shows how man, as the image of God, ought to be (Col. 1:15; Heb. 1:3). He enables us to remove sin and restore the true image of God.

Immanuel (im-MAN-you-el), sometimes written Emmanuel, is a name meaning "God with us." The prophet Isaiah foretold the coming of one who would be called Immanuel (Isa. 7:14). The gospel of Matthew tells us that Jesus is Immanuel, the long-awaited one who brings peace and salvation (Matt. 1:22-23).

immortality (im-or-TAL-ih-tee) refers to existence or life after death. The Bible teaches that just as God raised Jesus from death, he will also raise up his people after death (Ps. 16:9-11; Isa. 26:19; Luke 20:35-36; John 5:25-29; 1 Cor. 15; Phil. 3:21).

incarnation (in-car-NAY-shun) literally means "enfleshment," or "becoming flesh." It refers to the fact that God became man in Jesus. Or, as the apostle Paul says, "God was in Christ" (2 Cor. 5:19).

incense (IN-sens) is a sweet-smelling substance made of spices and gum. It was burned in ancient worship services, especially in ancient Israel (Lev. 10:1-7; Ps. 141:2).

inheritance (in-HEHR-ih-tans) means something inherited

—passed down from one generation to the next. The Israelites believed that the land they occupied was something given to them by God and must remain in their family (1 Kings 8:36). The firstborn son of a family received the birthright, which meant that he inherited a double portion of the family's goods but also the responsibility of caring for the females (Deut. 21:15-17). There were many other conditions placed on inheritance by Hebrew law (Num. 27:8-11; 36:6; Ruth 3:12-13).

In the New Testament the term "inheritance" is connected with the life and work of Jesus. As God's Son, he is the heir (Mark 12:7; Heb. 1:2). Believers in him are adopted sons, and therefore fellow-heirs (Rom. 8:17; Gal. 4:7). We have an "eternal inheritance," the kingdom of God (Matt. 25:34; Rom. 8:17-23; 1 Cor. 15:50; Heb. 9:15; 1 Pet. 1:3-4).

inspiration (in-spih-RAY-shun) (See p. 65.)

Isaac (EYE-zak) was the only son of Abraham and Sarah, born when Abraham was a hundred years old and Sarah was ninety (Gen. 17:17). Through Isaac, as God promised, the nation of Israel descended. Isaac had two sons, Jacob and Esau. It was Isaac's son Jacob who had twelve sons for whom the twelve tribes of Israel were named (Gen. 45:16, 28; Exod. 24:4).

Isaiah (eye-ZAY-uh) was one of the greatest of Israel's prophets. Little is known about his life. He was born in Jerusalem, probably of the family of some court official. He was married and had two children (2 Kings 19:2; Isa. 8:1, 3, 18). His name is very fitting to his prophecies, meaning "salvation of Jehovah." (See "Prophecy," p. 16.)

Ishmael (ISH-may-el) was the son of Abraham and Hagar,

Sarah's handmaid (Gen. 16). He was Isaac's older half-brother who became an archer. His descendants are the Ishmaelites (Gen. 21:14-21).

Israel (IZ-rah-el) is a term with four different but connected meanings. First, it is another name for Jacob, the father of the twelve tribes of the nation, Israel (Gen. 32:24-32). Second, it may refer to the twelve tribes as a nation (Gen. 47:27). Third, Israel was the name of the ten northern tribes when the two kingdoms were divided (1 Sam. 11:8). Finally, Israel may be used to refer to Christians, who are a "new Israel" or a new people of God (Gal. 6:16; see also ch. 4).

Issachar (IS-uh-kar) was one of the twelve sons of Jacob, and thus head of one of the twelve tribes (Gen. 30:17-18; Num. 26:23-24; see map B).

J

Jacob (JAY-kub) was the son of Isaac, Abraham's son, and was the younger twin of Esau. Jacob had two wives named Leah and Rachel. He was the father of twelve sons who became the ancestors of Israel's twelve tribes. He is also remembered for his dream of a ladder (Gen. 27:42–28:22) and for having wrestled with an angel of God (Gen. 32:24-32; see also ISRAEL).

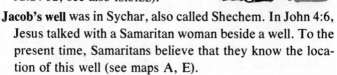

Jacob's well was in Sychar, also called Shechem. In John 4:6, Jesus talked with a Samaritan woman beside a well. To the present time, Samaritans believe that they know the location of this well (see maps A, E).

James was a popular Jewish name in the first century. There are at least three important men by the name of James in the New Testament. First, there is James the son of Zebedee, an apostle (Matt. 10:2). This James may have been Jesus' cousin. He was the older brother of the apostle John. He was killed by Herod Agrippa I (Acts 12:2). Second, there is James "the less," son of Alpheus, also an apostle (Matt. 10:3; Acts 1:13). Third, there is James who was the Lord's brother (Matt. 13:55). This James did not believe Jesus was the Messiah during his lifetime (John 7:5), but after Jesus' resurrection he accepted Jesus and became a leader in the Jerusalem church (Acts 12:17; 21:18). Tradition reports that he was killed by opponents to Christianity in A.D. 62. This James is generally thought to be the writer of the book of James in the New Testament (see "Letters," p. 23).

Japheth (JAY-feth) was one of the sons of Noah (Gen. 5:32) who had many descendants (Gen. 10:5).

Jebus (JEE-bus) (See JERUSALEM.)

Jehovah (jeh-HO-vuh) is one of the names of God. Out of respect for God, the Jews refused to write or pronounce his name. They wrote it without vowels, using only consonants, as YHWH. Later, Jews added the vowels of the Hebrew word for Lord and thus derived the name Jehovah or Yahweh (see YAHWEH; and "A Word for the Wise," p. 16).

Jephthah (JEF-thuh) was an early leader of Israel during the period of judges. He is chiefly re-membered for having made a rash promise to sacrifice the first one to meet him after a military victory. He was met by his only daughter,

whom he did sacrifice in spite of his grief (Judg. 11). For a long time, she was remembered each year as Jewish girls would spend four days out of the year mourning for her.

Jeremiah (JER-eh-MY-uh) was one of Israel's greatest prophets. He was the son of a priest. When he was called by God, Jeremiah protested that he was too young; but God assured him that he would provide the necessary strength for the job (Jer. 1). During the reign of King Jehoiakim, Jeremiah preached a great sermon in the Temple in which he aroused the anger of the king and the people so much that they plotted to take his life (Jer. 26). His prophecies are found in the Old Testament book of Jeremiah (see p. 17).

Jericho (JER-ih-ko) was a city near the Jordan River just north of the Dead Sea (see maps A, B, C, E). Actually, the city mentioned in the Old Testament (Josh. 6; 18:12, 21), the city of the New Testament (Luke 10:30), and the modern city are three different cities but are located near the same spot. The old Jericho was probably the oldest city in the world.

Jeroboam (JER-oh-BO-um) was the name of two kings of Israel. Jeroboam I was Israel's first king after the division of the nation, having been told by the prophet Ahijah that he would become king over ten tribes (1 Kings 11:29-40). He later built centers of idol worship for the people (1 Kings 12:25-33). Jeroboam II was Israel's thirteenth king, and he, too, allowed corruption and idol worship to abound during his reign (2 Kings 14:23-29).

Jerusalem (jer-OO-suh-lem), meaning "city of peace," was the capital of Israel before the division into the northern and southern empires (see maps A-E). It was the location of the Temple and the residence of Israel's kings. It was an old city in the time of the conquest (called "Jebus" at that time because it was in the possession of the Jebusites). It became Israel's capital only after David captured it in battle (2 Sam. 5:6-10).

As the center of Israel's life, home of both king and Temple, it is fitting that Jerusalem also played an important part in the birth of the church. Jesus preached and was crucified there. It was in Jerusalem that Peter preached the first Christian sermon and that the church was begun.

Jerusalem council: a meeting of early church leaders held in the city of Jerusalem. It is described in Acts 15. At this council Paul, Barnabas, Peter, and James all spoke and demonstrated to the others that God truly wanted all men to come to him and that it was not necessary for them first to become Jews and follow the Jewish customs. They made clear that the salvation of Christians was by the grace of God (Acts 15:9-11).

Jesse (JES-ee) was the grandson of Ruth and Boaz (Ruth 4:18-22). He had eight sons, the youngest of whom was David (1 Sam. 17:12-15), who became the great king and an ancestor of Jesus.

Jesus (JEE-zus) is a name meaning "Savior" (Matt. 1:21), which was given to the child born to Mary who was the Son of God (see ch. 5; "Christ," p. 90; and "Messiah," p. 96).

Jethro (JETH-row), also called Hobab, was a priest of Midian and Moses' father-in-law. After the exodus, Jethro advised Moses to appoint judges to handle disputes among the Israelites (Exod. 18:14-23).

Jew (JOO) originally referred to one who belonged to the tribe of Judah, one of Israel's twelve tribes. Later it came to refer to anyone of the Hebrew race (Matt. 2:2).

Jezebel (JEZ-uh-bel) was a wicked queen of the Northern Kingdom and the wife of King Ahab. She built an altar to the false god Baal in Samaria and had 450 priests. She killed God's true prophets and sought to kill the great prophet Elijah, whom God protected (1 Kings 18–19). Both Jezebel and her husband died terrible deaths (2 Kings 9:7, 30-37).

Joab (JO-ab) was David's commander-in-chief and a highly skilled general. But he was also very ruthless. It was Joab who killed David's rebel son Absalom against David's orders (2 Sam. 18:5, 9-15). Later, when David was old, Joab supported Adonijah, a rival with Solomon for the throne. He was killed on Solomon's orders for having shed innocent blood in the earlier killing of Abner and Amasa (1 Kings 2:28-35).

Job (JOBE) is the main character in the Old Testament book of Job (see p. 15). Job suffered much but never lost his faith in God although he did not understand all the reasons for suffering.

Joel (JO-uhl) was one of Israel's great prophets whose personal life is largely unknown. His prophecies are found in the Old Testament book of Joel (see p. 17).

John was a popular name in New Testament times. Two men

by the name are important in the New Testament. First, John the Baptist was Jesus' cousin. He lived a rugged life in the desert and preached the coming of the expected Jewish Messiah. He prepared the way for Jesus and his ministry. John the Baptist was put to death by Herod Antipas (Luke 1:3; Matt. 3:13-17; 14:6-12).

Second, John the apostle was one of the three apostles closest to Jesus (with Peter and James). He was probably a fisherman and was the brother of the apostle James (Mark 1:19-20). He wrote the fourth gospel, the three letters of John, and the book of Revelation (see "Gospels," p. 21; "Letters," p. 23; and "Prophecy," p. 27).

John Mark (See MARK.)

Jonah (JO-nuh) was an early prophet of Israel. It was his work to preach to the Gentiles in Nineveh. He is chiefly remembered for having tried to run away from his task and having been swallowed by a great fish for three days (see p. 18).

Jonathan (JON-uh-thun) was the oldest son of King Saul and a friend of David. More than once he risked his life for David, and he is remembered as a great example of true friendship. Jonathan, his brothers, and his father, Saul, were all killed in battle against the Philistines on Mount Gilboa (1 Sam. 14:49; 18:1-4; 19:1-7; 23:16; 31:2).

Joppa (JOP-uh) is an ancient city on the coast of Palestine (see maps A, B, C, E). In Joppa, Peter raised Tabitha (Acts 9:36-42) and had the vision of the sheet filled with animals (Acts 10:9-16).

Jordan (JOR-dun): the only large river in Palestine (see maps A, B, C, E). It is often mentioned in both the Old and the New Testaments. The Israelites crossed the Jordan into the promised land after the death of Moses (Deut. 3:20, 25, 27; Josh. 3–4).

Joseph (JO-zef) is the name of several men in the Bible, but two are especially important. First, there was Joseph the eleventh son of Jacob. He was Jacob's favorite son and was given a beautiful coat by his father. He was sold into Egypt as a slave by his jealous brothers, who reported to his father that he had been killed by wild beasts. He was a noble man, kind and forgiving whether in times of trouble or later when he was in the position of ruling Egypt. Joseph became the father of two of the twelve tribes, through his sons Manasseh and Ephraim (see map B). His story is told in Genesis 30:22-24 and Genesis 37–50.

Second, there was Joseph the husband of Jesus' mother, Mary. He was a carpenter, living in Nazareth and a descendant of King David. He was warned in a dream that Herod was plotting to take the infant Jesus' life, and so he fled into Egypt. Because little is said about Joseph during Jesus' ministry and because Jesus on the cross gave his mother into John's care, it is often assumed that Joseph died either before or during Jesus' ministry. Matthew 1 and Luke 2 and 3 tell us most of what we know about this Joseph.

Joshua (JOSH-you-uh) was Moses' assistant and a great general. After Moses' death, Joshua became the Israelite leader during the conquest of the land of Canaan (Exod. 17:9; Deut. 31; Josh. 1). The Old Testament book of Joshua, named for him, tells the story of the conquest (see p. 13).

Josiah (jo-SIGH-uh) was king of Judah for thirty-one years.

He was a good king and tried to call the people of Judah back to God. He was killed in battle at Megiddo in 609 B.C. (2 Kings 22–23; 2 Chron. 34–35).

jot is the smallest letter in the Hebrew language, looking about like an apostrophe sign ('). It is used as a figure of speech for something very small (Matt. 5:17-18).

joy in the Bible means much more than just happiness. It is a feeling of well being, which does not depend on pleasant circumstances or happenings. For example, Paul and Silas were able to feel joy in prison (Acts 16:23-33). Joy is one of the fruits of the Spirit (Gal. 5:22-23).

Jubilee (JOO-bi-LEE) means a joyous celebration. The Old Testament book of Leviticus says that every fiftieth year in Israel was to be called a jubilee year. In this special year, all Israelites who were in bondage to their fellow Israelites were to be freed. All family properties which had been sold were to be returned, and the land was to remain uncultivated. The people were to live very simply on crops stored from the previous year and on what happened to grow without cultivation (Lev. 25).

Judah (JOO-duh) was the fourth son of Jacob and Leah. Little is known about his life. It was Judah who talked his brothers into selling Joseph instead of killing him (Gen. 37:26-28). As one of Jacob's twelve sons, Judah is the father of one of the twelve tribes of Israel (see map B). David was of the tribe of Judah.

Judah was also the name of the Southern Kingdom after Israel became divided into two separate kingdoms about 912 B.C. As a nation, Judah lasted until 587 B.C., when it was conquered by Babylon. At that time, Jerusalem, the capital of Judah, was destroyed and many Jews were carried off into captivity. (See also "Kingdom and Exile," p. 36.)

Judas Iscariot (JOO-dus is-KARE-ee-ut) is remembered as the apostle who betrayed Jesus with a kiss. He received thirty pieces of silver for helping Jesus' enemies (Matt. 26:47-50; 27:3-10). After betraying Jesus, Judas repented and hanged himself (Matt. 27:3-5).

Jude (JOOD) was one of the brothers of Jesus who, like James, apparently did not accept Jesus as Messiah during his ministry, but later did (John 7:5; Jude 1). He wrote the book of Jude in the New Testament.

Judea (joo-DEE-uh) is used in the Bible to refer to the land of the Jews who returned from the Babylonian exile, since most of them were of the tribe of Judah. It is also used as the name of a district of the Persian Empire which was usually governed by a Jew (Ezra 5:8; Hag. 1:14; 2:2). In New Testament times, it referred to a district of Palestine, part of the Roman Empire (see map E).

Judges (See p. 13.)

judgment (JUJ-ment) is used in the Old Testament to mean a type of punishment God brings upon his people to instruct and purify them (Isa. 2:12; Amos 5:18; Hos. 5:8-9). In the New Testament, the term is also used for the unkind and self-righteous way some people criticize and condemn others. Jesus warned against this kind of judgment (Matt. 7:1). The final judgment spoken of in the New Testament (Matt. 1:2-14; John 16:11; Rom. 2:16) refers to that time when the world will be destroyed and Christ will reign completely as Lord over all.

justification (JUS-tih-fih-KAY-shun) means a making right or righteous and is an action of God toward those who have faith in him (Acts 13:38-39, KJV; Rom. 3:24-26; 4:5-8). It includes forgiveness and a declaration of freedom from guilt which brings man into a new standing before God.

K

Kenites (KEE-nites): one of the peoples of Canaan during the time of Abraham (Gen. 15:19; see map A). Moses' father-in-law was a Kenite, and they helped Israel find its way during the exodus. Later, the Kenites became part of the tribe of Judah. It was Jael, the wife of Heber the Kenite, who killed Sisera the Canaanite general (Judg. 4).

Keturah (ke-TYOO-ruh) was Abraham's second wife (Gen. 25:1). Abraham married her after Sarah, the mother of Isaac, died. She had six sons from whom the Arabian tribes descended (Gen. 25:2-6).

Kidron (KID-ron) is the name of a valley which runs east of Jerusalem twenty miles to the Dead Sea. It was a burial place and a place for dumping idols of false gods (1 Kings 15:13; 2 Kings 23:6). When David's rebel son, Absalom, seized the throne, David fled across the Kidron valley to escape (2 Sam. 15:23). Centuries later, Jesus crossed it on the way to Gethsemane (John 18:1).

Kingdom of God may mean two different but closely connected things. First, it may refer to the people who are governed by God's will (Rev. 5:10). Second, it may refer to God's reign or rule. God, as creator of the entire universe, has always ruled the universe in a special sense. But in Jesus' life, death, and resurrection, God's rule breaks into history in a different sense as men and women accept his will for their individual lives (Matt. 6:33; Mark 10:15).

Kings, 1 and 2 (See p. 14.)

Korah (KO-ruh) was an Israelite who, with Dathan and Abiram, led a rebellion against Moses' leadership. Korah and many followers were swallowed up into the earth (Num. 26:10).

L

Laban (LAY-ban) was Abraham's nephew and the brother of Rebekah, Isaac's wife. He is remembered largely for the craftiness he showed when Isaac's son Jacob (Laban's nephew) was tricked into working several years in order to take Rachel as his wife (Gen. 29).

lamb in the Bible is first of all a young sheep (Exod. 12:3-6; Deut. 32:14). They were important in the Old Testament because they were often used for sacrifices (Gen. 4:4; 22:7; Exod. 29:38-42). Especially important for the nation of Israel was the Passover lamb, after whose sacrifice they were delivered from slavery in Egypt (Exod. 12:3-6).

This Passover lamb, or lamb of God, became a symbol to Israel of redemption from sin (1 Cor. 5:7). Thus Jesus was called the Lamb of God by John the Baptist (John 1:29, 36) and the apostle John used the lamb as a symbol for Christ many times in the book of Revelation.

Lamentations (See p. 17.)

Laodicea (lay-ODD-ih-SEE-uh) was a wealthy city in Asia Minor (see maps F, G). It was on one of the great trade routes of the time. The New Testament book of Revelation strongly criticizes the church at Laodicea (Rev. 3:14-22). In his letter to the church at Colossae the apostle Paul refers to a letter he wrote to the Laodicean church (Col. 4:16). It is not known whether this letter is actually lost or can be identified as one of the letters presently in the New Testament.

law is a term often used to refer to the Ten Commandments which were given to Israel through Moses (Exod. 20:3-17). It also is sometimes used to refer to the first five books of the Old Testament (see p. 11). The Law was given by God because of his love, and so man might know God's will. In Christ, however, God has shown his love and will for man in an even clearer way (Heb. 1:1-2).

laying on of hands was a gesture often used in ancient times to symbolize a special appointment or grace. For example, when a father placed his hands on his child's head it symbolized the fact that the child would inherit his father's possessions. The ceremony also symbolized the rights and responsibilities of an office, just as we have ceremonies for installing government officials today. In the New Testament the laying on of hands symbolized the Holy Spirit's selection of Paul and Barnabas to preach to the Gentiles (Acts 13:3).

Lazarus (LAZ-uh-rus) was the brother of Martha and Mary and a friend of Jesus. The gospel of John tells how Lazarus died while Jesus was away, but upon his return Jesus raised Lazarus from the tomb (John 11). This miracle shows us both Jesus' power over death and his love for us.

Leah (LEE-uh) was the daughter of Laban, the sister of Rachel, and the wife of Jacob (Gen. 29:21-30). She was the mother of six of the twelve sons of Jacob, the father of the twelve tribes of Israel (Gen. 35:23).

leaven (LEV-en) is a substance used in baking to make bread rise. Its use was forbidden in the bread baked for Passover (Lev. 2:11; Exod. 12). Jesus and his disciples were eating unleavened bread the night he was betrayed (Matt. 26:17-20).

letters (See EPISTLES.)

Levi (LEE-vie) was Jacob's third son by Leah and the father of the priestly tribe of Israel (Gen. 29:34; see LEVITES). Levi is also one of the names of the apostle Matthew.

Levites (LEE-vites) are descendants of Levi, one of the twelve sons of Jacob. They were the priestly tribe who performed such duties as carrying the tabernacle and offering sacrifices. The Levites received no tribal territory, but forty-eight cities were assigned to them (Num. 35). Those Levites who were priests were supported by offerings (Lev. 27:30-33).

Leviticus (See p. 12.)

levy (LEV-ee) is a tax or tribute. In the Old Testament, this word is also used for service rendered, such as labor. King Solomon levied a service period of four months per year on some 30,000 Israelites (1 Kings 5:13-14).

Lights, Feast of (See DEDICATION, FEAST OF.)

lintel (LIN-t'l) is the wooden beam or stone which forms the top of a doorway. In Egypt, on the night of the first Passover, the lintel was marked to identify God's people (Exod. 12:22-23).

lord is a term expressing honor, power, and authority. It can mean a merely human martyr or ruler, but in the Bible it refers especially to God and Jesus. Generally, Jesus is called Lord as he now reigns over the whole creation and is Lord of the Christian's life (1 Cor. 6:11). Christians are those who recognize Christ as Lord, confess his name as Lord (Rom. 10:9), and obey his will in all parts of life. (See "Lord and Christ," p. 49.)

Lord's Prayer is a name often given to a prayer of Jesus, also sometimes called the "Disciples' Prayer." The gospels report that Jesus' disciples asked him to teach them to pray. This prayer was given as a model in answer to their request (Matt. 6:9-13; Luke 11:2-4).

Lord's supper (See p. 94.)

Lot was Abraham's nephew who went with him to settle in Canaan (Gen. 11:27-32). He settled near the wicked city of Sodom and was rescued from the city before God destroyed it. Lot was both selfish and unwise, and suffered greatly from having chosen to live in a wicked place (Gen. 13–14).

love (See p. 95.)

love feast was a meal eaten by first-century Christians in connection with the Lord's Supper to express their fellowship and brotherly love (1 Cor. 11:18-22).

Lucifer (LOO-sih-fer) is another name for Satan from a description of the king of Babylon in Isaiah 14:12 (KJV).

Luke is the writer of the third gospel (see "Gospels," p. 21) and the Acts of the Apostles (see "History" p. 23). Luke, a well-educated physician, was a Gentile and a traveling companion of the apostle Paul.

Lydia (LID-ee-uh) was the first person converted to Christianity by Paul in Europe. She was a businesswoman in Philippi who had already worshiped God before she heard about Jesus Christ. After her conversion the first church in Philippi met at her house (Acts 16:14-15, 40).

Lystra (LIS-truh) was a city of Asia Minor (see maps F, G) visited by Paul several times in his missionary travels (Acts 14:6). Timothy came from Lystra (Acts 16:1).

M

Macedonia (MAS-eh-DOH-nee-uh) is an area north of Greece and a Roman province in New Testament times (see maps F, G). Paul visited Macedonia often (Acts 16:9-12; 17:1-15; 20:1-6).

magic (MAJ-ik) gets its name from a priestly group of the Persians, the Magi, who were very religious. The term came to mean anything which attempted to control the natural forces of the universe or to use the forces of an invisible world. Most of the people who attempted to practice magic were interested in personal gain, and they often used other people in unfair ways. Examples of such magicians in the New Testament are Simon (Acts 8:9), Elymas (Acts 13:8), and the sons of Sceva (Acts 19:14).

Malachi (See p. 19.)

mammon (MAM-un) is an Aramaic word for riches. Jesus said that some people wrongly see mammon as the whole goal of their lives (Matt. 6:24).

Manasseh (muh-NAS-uh) was the oldest son of Joseph. He and his brother Ephraim each became the head of one of the twelve tribes of Israel (Josh. 17:7-10; see map B). He was born while Joseph was in Egypt (Gen. 48:5).

There was also an evil king of Judah named Manasseh who persecuted those who were faithful to God (2 Kings 21:1-6) and was eventually carried captive into Babylon (2 Chron. 33:11).

manger (MAIN-jer) is a stall or a trough for cattle. Luke tells us that Jesus was laid in a manger when he was born (Luke 2:7).

manna (MAN-uh) was a special food which God provided for his people during the exodus from Egypt. It fell at night and resembled dew drops. It was white and good-tasting (Exod. 16:2, 11-26).

mantle (MAN-t'l): a large, robelike outer garment without sleeves (1 Kings 19:18-19).

maranatha (MAIR-uh-NATH-uh) is an Aramaic expression which was used by early Christians. It means either "our Lord comes" or "come, Lord!" (see 1 Cor. 16:22).

Mark is sometimes called John Mark in the New Testament. He was the writer of the second gospel. When the Jerusalem Christians were first persecuted, Peter, on leaving prison, went to the home of John Mark's mother where many Christians were praying for him (Acts 12:12). Later, Paul and Barnabas took Mark with them on their first missionary journey (Acts 13:5). Tradition tells us that Mark wrote his gospel with the aid of the apostle Peter (see "Gospels," p. 21).

Martha (MAR-thuh) was the sister of Lazarus and Mary of Bethany, friends of Jesus (Luke 10:38-42).

martyr (MAR-ter) originally meant "witness," but came to mean those who were killed for giving witness to Jesus Christ. The first Christian martyr was Stephen (Acts 22:20).

Mary was a popular name in New Testament days as today, and there are several important women by that name. Best known is Jesus' mother, wife of Joseph. She stood at the foot of the cross at Jesus' crucifixion and was entrusted by him to John (John 19:25-27).

There is also Mary Magdalene, a woman from whom Jesus cast seven demons. She followed Jesus' body to the grave and was the first to learn of the resurrection (Matt. 28:1-8).

Finally, there was Mary the sister of Martha and Lazarus, friends of Jesus in Bethany. She is also remembered for having anointed Jesus' feet (John 12:1-8).

Matthew (MATH-you), also called Levi, was the son of Alpheus and a tax collector. He was one of Jesus' twelve apostles (Mark 2:14) and the writer of the first gospel (see "Gospels," p. 21).

Matthias (muh-THIE-us) was the man chosen to take the place of Judas among the apostles after Jesus' resurrection (Acts 1:15-26). Like the others, he had been a follower of Jesus during his ministry (Acts 1:21-22).

mediator (ME-dee-ay-ter): one who restores friendship between those who have become enemies (1 Sam. 2:25). Jesus is the mediator between man and God, restoring our relationship with God (1 Tim. 2:5; Heb. 8:6; 9:15).

Mediterranean Sea (MED-ih-tuh-RAY-nee-un) is the name of the large body of water south of eastern Europe and western Asia (see maps F, G). In the Bible it is often called "the sea" or "the great sea" (Num. 13:29; Josh. 1:4).

Melchizedek (mel-KIZ-uh-dek) was a priest and king of Salem. He blessed Abraham in the name of God and received contributions from Abraham (Gen. 14:18-20).

mercy is compassion which causes one to help those who are poor or weak. It is one of the qualities or characteristics of true followers of Jesus Christ (Matt. 5:7; James 2:1-13).

Mesopotamia (MES-oh-poh-TAME-ee-uh) is the name for the region between the Tigris and Euphrates rivers (see map D). It was about where modern Iraq is today. In the Old Testament, it is sometimes called Aram (Gen. 24:10; Deut. 23:4; 1 Chron. 19:6). Babylonia and Assyria were in the central and southern part of Mesopotamia.

Messiah (See "Lord and Christ," pp. 49 and 96.)

Methuselah (me-THOO-zeh-luh) lived before the great flood. He was the son of Enoch and the father of Lamech, and he lived 969 years (Gen. 5:21-27).

Micah (See p. 18.)

Michael (MY-k'l), which means "who is like God," is the name of an angel whose chief responsibility was the care of God's people (Dan. 10:13, 21).

Midianites (MID-ee-un-ites) were people descended from Midian, a son of Abraham by his second wife (Gen. 25:1-6; 37:25, 36). During the time of Moses they were nomads, or people who constantly traveled about, but they were very wealthy (Num. 31:2, 32-34).

minister (MIN-is-ter) originally meant anyone who serves another, but came to have the special meaning of one who lives in service to God and others. Priests and Levites were ministers (Exod. 28:43; Num. 3:31), as was Paul when he took the gospel to the Gentiles (Rom. 15:16).

miracle (MERE-ih-k'l) means a special event which cannot be explained apart from God's action. Miracles are signs pointing to God's mighty power through which he loves man. The Bible tells us of many miracles, but we see them especially in Jesus' life. There they point to the fact that Jesus was God's Son (John 20:31). And, because they were mostly healing miracles, they point to God's love for his creation (Mark 10:45).

The greatest miracle in the Bible, however, is Jesus' resurrection from the grave. In this miracle, God shows his love for Jesus and his power over death (1 Cor. 15:56-57).

missionary (MISH-un-air-ee): one who journeys about to take the gospel to other places. Paul and Barnabas were the first Christian missionaries (Acts 13:1-3; see also "The Missionary Church," p. 56).

Moabites (MO-uh-bites) were people descended from Abraham's nephew Lot, who lived east of the Jordan (Num. 21:13-15; see maps A-E). They refused to let the Israelites through their land to reach Canaan (Judg. 11:17-18) and continued to have troubled relations with Israel for many years (Num. 22–24; 2 Sam. 8; Isa. 15–16).

Moloch or **Molech** (MO-lock or MO-leck) was the name of a heathen false god, worshiped especially by the Ammonites through such practices as the sacrifice of children (Lev. 18:21; 20:1-5).

Mordecai (MOR-deh-kie) was a Jewish leader in the book of Esther. He and Queen Esther became famous for saving the Jewish people from a plot to destroy them by the evil chief officer of Persia, Haman (Esth. 2–10).

Moriah (mo-RYE-uh) was the mountain where God told Abraham to offer Isaac as a sacrifice (Gen. 22:2). Later, Solomon built a temple on Mount Moriah (2 Chron. 3:1; see 1 Chron. 21:15–22:1). Its location is uncertain.

Moses (MO-zez) is one of the greatest men of the Old Testament. He spent the first forty years of his life in Pharaoh's court (Exod. 2:1-10). Later he was called by God in a burning bush (Exod. 3:2-3) to bring his people out of Egypt in the exodus. He and his brother Aaron, the spokesman, asked the Egyptian Pharaoh to let the Israelites go. After ten terrible plagues, the Israelites were finally allowed to leave.

It was through Moses that God gave the Ten Commandments to his people (Exod. 20). After Moses' death, Joshua became the leader of Israel during the first years of the period of conquest of the promised land.

Mount of Olives (See OLIVES, MOUNT OF.)

mystery (MIS-ter-ee) is a word not found in the Old Testament, but it occurs numerous times in the New Testament.

Some of the pagan religions of the time used it to mean something obscure or unknown to most people. Paul borrowed this term to teach that the "mystery," or divine truth, was now made clear to all men in Christ Jesus (Rom. 16:25-26; Eph. 3:3-6; Col. 1:26). All men can now see God's purpose and his love for mankind in the gospel (Rom. 16:25).

N

Naaman (NAY-uh-mun) was a commander of the army of the king of Syria. He suffered from the terrible disease of leprosy. A young slave girl told him of the great prophet Elisha, who healed him by telling him to dip himself seven times in the Jordan River. Because of his cure, Naaman acknowledged the God of Israel as the only God (2 Kings 5:1-27).

Naboth (NAY-bahth) was an Israelite who owned a vineyard near the palace of King Ahab. The king wanted Naboth's vineyard so much that he and his wife Jezebel had Naboth killed so that they could take it (1 Kings 21). Later, Ahab, Jezebel, and their son were all punished for their sin against Naboth (1 Kings 22:24-40; 2 Kings 8:25–9:37).

Nahum (See p. 18.)

Naomi (nay-OH-mee) was the mother-in-law of Ruth. After the death of her son (Ruth's husband), Naomi returned from Moab with Ruth and there advised her daughter-in-law in her courtship with Boaz. This story is told in the Old Testament book of Ruth.

Naphtali (NAF-tuh-lie) was the sixth of Jacob's twelve sons and thus also the head of one of Israel's twelve tribes (Gen. 35:23-26; see map B).

Nathan (NAY-thun) was a prophet and also a trusted advisor to King David. It was through Nathan that God prevented David from building a Temple (2 Sam. 7). It was Nathan who brought the message of God's displeasure at David's sin in taking Bathsheba, the wife of Uriah (2 Sam. 12). Later, it was Nathan's watchfulness that discovered a plot to prevent David's son Solomon from taking the throne (1 Kings 1:8-53). Thus Nathan was a faithful prophet and also a close friend of both David and his son Solomon.

Nathanael (nuh-THAN-ay-el) was one of Jesus' disciples who is mentioned only in the gospel of John (John 1:45-49). It has been suggested that he might be the Bartholomew mentioned in the synoptic gospels.

Nazarene (NAZ-uh-reen) means a person who lived in the town of Nazareth. Jesus lived there as a child, and he was often called a Nazarene, probably by both his friends and enemies (Matt. 2:23; 26:71; Acts 2:22). And, because they were followers of Jesus, Christians were often called Nazarenes as well (Acts 24:5).

Nazareth (NAZ-uh-reth) was a small town in southern Galilee (see map E). It was the town where Joseph and Mary lived after returning from Egypt to protect the baby Jesus (Luke 1:26; 2:4).

Nazarite (NAZ-uh-rite): a Jew who took a special vow of commitment to God. The vow required one to let his hair grow long, deny himself certain foods and drink, and observe special religious ceremonies. The apostle Paul may have taken such a vow (Acts 18:8; 21:23-26).

Nebo (NEE-bow) was the mountain near the Dead Sea (see

maps A, B, C, E) from which Moses saw the promised land (Deut. 34:1).

Nebuchadnezzar or **Nebuchadrezzar** (NEB-you-kad-NEZ-er or NEB-you-kad-REZ-er) was the greatest king of Babylon. He was the founder of the New Babylonian Empire and ruled from 604 to 561 B.C. (2 Kings 25:1-26). Nebuchadnezzar built the city of Babylon into one of the wonders of the world. It had three walls around it and a water-filled moat. He also built many pagan temples.

Nehemiah (NEE-huh-MY-uh) was one of the leaders of the return from Babylonian captivity when the city of Jerusalem was rebuilt and its fallen walls restored in only fifty-two days (Neh. 6:15). He was a good leader and cooperated with Ezra in bringing about a general reform. His story is told in the book that bears his name (see p. 15).

Nero (NEE-row) was the fifth Roman emperor. He was born in A.D. 37 and began ruling in the year 54. During the first few years of his reign, he was a good ruler, and it was possibly in this period that the apostle Paul was brought before him and dismissed (Acts 25:10-11). Later, however, Nero became very evil. He murdered his own mother and many of his closest friends. In A.D. 64, the city of Rome was largely destroyed in a  great fire. Although the fire was blamed on Christians, many people suspected Nero of having started the fire. Many Christians, probably including the apostles Paul and Peter, were killed in the following persecution. In the summer of A.D. 68, Nero took his own life.

New Testament: God's promise to save those who trust and obey Christ, in contrast to the "Old Testament" of salvation through the law of Moses. The term also came to refer to the 27 books of inspired early Christian writings. A "testament" is best understood as a covenant or binding agreement. The writers of the Old Testament looked forward to a new covenant with God. Jesus himself describes his life and death as God's new covenant with men (1 Cor. 11:25). The New Testament writings tell us about this new covenant which Christ brings to men. (See also "Covenant," p. 91; and ch. 3.)

Nicodemus (NICK-oh-DEE-mus) was a leading Pharisee and one of the Jewish rulers in the Sanhedrin. To avoid being seen with Jesus, Nicodemus came to him by night and was told that a man must be "born again" (John 3:1-15). Later, when there was a plot to kill Jesus, Nicodemus spoke out against condemning him without a fair trial (John 7:25-44). Finally, after Jesus' death, Nicodemus openly showed his loyalty for Jesus by assisting in the burial (John 19:38-42).

Nile is the name of the great river of Egypt and one of the longest in the world, running 4,050 miles into Africa (see maps D, F, G). It was in the Nile that the baby Moses was hidden and found by Pharaoh's daughter (Exod. 2:3-10).

Nimrod (NIM-rod) was a hunter and builder in the Old Testament who founded the city of Nineveh (Gen. 10:8-12; 1 Chron. 1:10).

Nineveh (NIN-uh-vuh) was one of the oldest cities of the world. It was to Nineveh that the prophet Jonah was sent to warn the people to turn from their wickedness (Jon. 3:4). The ruins of Nineveh have been discovered by archaeologists (see map D).

Noah (NO-uh) was a righteous man in a wicked age (Gen. 6:1-13). God warned Noah that he would destroy the world by water. He gave Noah instructions for the building of a large boat or ark, so that he and his family might be saved. Genesis 6–9 tells the story of the flood that followed. After it was over, God promised Noah that he would never again send a universal flood (Gen. 9:9-17). All men are descendants of Noah, but Christians remember him because of his great faith and trust in God (Heb. 11:7).

Numbers (See p. 13.)

O

oath means a promise which appeals to the truth of a statement by calling on a person or thing as a witness. For example, one might say something like, "I give you my word as these mountains now witness." Jesus, however, taught against the careless use of oaths. He taught that we should say simply "yes" and "no" and tell the truth all the time without having to say special oaths (Matt. 5:33-37).

Obadiah (See p. 18.)

obedience (oh-BEE-dee-ens) means respecting and honoring authority, whether that of man or God, and doing what is asked or commanded. Christians are to be obedient to God as Jesus Christ was (Phil. 2:8).

offerings (OFF-er-ingz) were commanded by God in the Old Testament to show trust and commitment to him. Special offerings consisted of various things such as animals and grain (Lev. 4:1-35; 6:24-30). These offerings were gifts, not because God needs anything, but in order to demonstrate that he is worthy and that we should place him first. The

New Testament shows that Christians also make offerings. But instead of giving God animals or other gifts, they give him their lives by dedicating all of their thoughts and actions to God (Rom. 12:1-2).

oil in the Bible almost always refers to olive oil. Sometimes oil was used as a medicine (Ps. 23:5), and sometimes it was used for cooking (Exod. 29:2) or as a cosmetic (Ps. 104:15), but quite often it was used in ceremonies where special men were anointed with oil to signify some special task or honor. Priests, prophets, and kings were anointed in this manner (Exod. 28:41; 1 Kings 19:15-16).

Old Testament: God's promise of special blessings to the Jews. Christians use the term to refer to ancient Israel's holy writings, the thirty-nine inspired books of the "Old Testament" in our Bibles. The term "testament" is best understood as a covenant or binding agreement. For Christians, these books are called "old" because they look forward to the "new" covenant which God made with man through Jesus Christ. (See also ch. 2 and "Covenant," p. 91.)

Olives, Mount of: a ridge east of the city of Jerusalem, about one mile long with four small peaks on it. Jesus passed over the Mount of Olives as he made the triumphant entry into Jerusalem (Luke 19:37). It was in the garden of Gethsemane on the side of this mountain that Jesus prayed and was taken captive before his crucifixion (Matt. 26:30-50).

omega (oh-MAY-guh or oh-MEE-guh) is the name of the last letter of the Greek alphabet (see ALPHA).

omnipotence (om-NIP-oh-tents) is a word used to describe God. This word is not found in the Bible but points to the biblical truth that God is all-powerful and has the ability to do whatever he wills (Deut. 4:37; 1 Chron. 29:12). Because he is good, however, he does not will to do anything foolish or evil.

omnipresence (OM-nih-PREZ-ents) means being everywhere at once. Like "omnipotence," it is not found in the Bible, but it has been used to describe God. It means that he is everywhere in the universe. There is no place where God is not present (Ps. 139:7-12).

omniscience (om-NISH-ens) means all-knowing. Like omnipotence and omnipresence, it is not found in the Bible but is clearly taught (Ps. 147:5). It means that God knows all things perfectly—past, present, and future. He knows us even better than we know ourselves. It must be remembered, however, that to say that God knows all things does not mean that he causes all things to happen.

Omri (OM-ree) was the sixth king of the Northern Empire, Israel. He was a capable but ruthless soldier (1 Kings 16:15-28). He was the father of King Ahab, who married the wicked Jezebel.

Onesimus (oh-NES-ih-mus), whose name means "profitable," was the slave of an early Christian named Philemon. Apparently, Onesimus robbed his master and made his way to Rome where he became a Christian and was persuaded by Paul to return to his master. The little letter titled *Philemon* in the New Testament is the apostle Paul's letter to Onesimus' master explaining what had happened in Rome and asking Philemon to receive Onesimus back with kindness and as a Christian brother.

ordain (or-DANE) basically means to set apart for a special work. Just as there is a special ceremony or inauguration for the president of the United States, there was in ancient times an ordination ceremony for many special offices. In the book of Acts we read of Paul and Barnabas being "set aside" or ordained for special missionary work. In the early church, this often involved prayer, fasting, and the laying on of hands (Acts 13:2-3; 14:23; 1 Tim. 4:14; 2 Tim. 1:6).

ordination (OR-dih-NAY-shun) is the ceremony in which one is ordained for a special task.

ostraka (OS-tra-kuh): pieces of broken pottery. Long ago paper and other writing materials were scarce, and children often used these pieces of pottery to do written exercises on. Adults also wrote short notes and letters on ostraka. Recent archaeological discoveries disclosed a number of important and interesting writings made on ostraka.

Othniel (OTH-nee-uhl) was the first of Israel's judges to drive out foreign oppressors. After Joshua's death, Mesopotamia conquered Israel. At that time, in answer to prayer, Othniel defeated the Mesopotamians and brought about a peace for forty years while he reigned as judge (Judg. 3:7-11).

P

Palestine (PAL-es-tine): an area some seventy miles wide and one hundred fifty miles long on the eastern shore of the Mediterranean Sea (see map E). The name probably comes from the Philistines who occupied the coastal areas at an early date. Palestine is a general name for the whole area which in Bible times was first called Canaan (Gen. 12:5), then Israel (1 Sam. 13:19), and later Judea.

pantheism (PAN-thee-izm) (See p. 30.)

Paphos (PAY-fos) was the capital city of the island of Cyprus (see maps F, G). Paul and Barnabas visited this city and taught the Christian message in the court of Sergius Paulus. They were opposed by a magician named Elymas (Acts 13:6-13).

papyrus (puh-PIE-rus) is a plant which grows in lakes and swampy areas. These plants were used in making a sort of paper on which ancient men wrote. At one time, the books of the Bible were all written on papyrus and were rolled on scrolls.

parable (PAIR-uh-b'l) is a type of story which teaches a lesson. Parables were among Jesus' favorite ways of teaching. An example of a parable is the story of the good Samaritan (Luke 10:29-37).

paraclete (PAIR-uh-kleet) is the English spelling of a Greek word for one who speaks for the cause of another. Jesus uses this word to refer to the Holy Spirit (John 14:16, 26), and it is also used to mean Christ himself (1 John 2:1). The word is translated "advocate," "comforter," and "counselor."

paradise (PAIR-uh-dize) refers to heaven. The word is found only three times in the New Testament (Luke 23:43; 2 Cor. 12:3; Rev. 2:7).

Passover (PASS-oh-ver) refers first to the time when the death angel passed over the homes of the Israelites, not killing their firstborn, when the tenth and last plague was visited on

Egypt (Exod. 12:1-36). Thus it became the name of the annual Jewish feast which celebrated this event (Lev. 23:5-8).

Pastoral Epistles (See "Letters," pp. 23-24.)

patience (PAY-shents) means endurance in face of trials and on behalf of others. It is one of the characteristics Christians should have, according to Paul (Gal. 5:22-23).

Patmos (PAT-mus) is a very small island off the coast of Asia Minor in the Aegean Sea. It is about twenty-eight miles south of Samos (see maps, F,G) and about sixteen square miles in area. According to tradition, the apostle John was banished to the Isle of Patmos for eighteen months and while there received the vision now recorded in the book of Revelation.

patriarch (PAY-tree-ark) is a term describing the men who founded the Hebrew race and nation. Such men as Abraham, Jacob, and Isaac are among the great patriarchs (Acts 7:8, 9; Heb. 7:4).

Paul was the great apostle to the Gentiles. He is one of the main characters of the book of Acts, which describes his mission efforts and imprisonment (see especially Acts 13–28). The New Testament contains thirteen letters by Paul (see "Letters, " pp. 23-26).

Paul was a dedicated Jew who had persecuted Christians before his con-version (Acts 9), his Hebrew name having been Saul. But afterward, he was one of the most devoted fol-lowers and preachers of Christ in the early church. He was made the thir-teenth apostle, the only one who was not a disciple of Christ's during his ministry. Tradition tells us that he was beheaded just outside of Rome (See also "The Missionary Church," p. 56; and "The Writings of the Church," p. 59).

Paulus, Sergius (PAW-lus, SUR-jee-us) was the Roman official on the island of Cyprus when Paul and Barnabas visited there on their first missionary journey. The book of Acts tells us that Sergius Paulus believed (Acts 13:4-13).

peace is sometimes a word of greeting in the Bible (Gen. 43:23, KJV), or it may describe a time without war or turmoil (Num. 6:26; Acts 9:31). But mostly it means the calm spirit that can be enjoyed through faith in Christ (Rom. 5:21; Phil. 4:6-7; Col. 1:20).

Pentateuch (PEN-tuh-tyook) is the name given to the first five books of the Old Testament: Genesis, Exodus, Leviticus, Numbers, and Deuteronomy (see "Law," p. 11).

Pentecost (PEN-teh-kost): a Jewish feast celebrating the first fruits of the harvest (Exod. 34:22; Deut. 16:9-11). Christians remember Pentecost as the occasion when Peter and the apostles were strengthened by the Holy Spirit and began preaching the gospel. On that first day, the book of Acts reports that three thousand became Christians (Acts 2).

Perga (PUR-guh) was a city in Asia Minor (see maps F, G) through which Paul and Barnabas passed on at least two occasions (Acts 13:13-14; 14:24-25). It was at Perga that John Mark separated from the group and returned to Jerusalem.

persecute (PUR-seh-KYOOT): to attack someone in ridicule and intolerance. The Old Testament tells of numerous occasions when God's people were persecuted (Deut. 30:7; Jer. 15:15; Lam. 5:1-9). The early Christians suffered persecution from the Romans because they would not worship the Roman emperor (Acts 8:1; Gal. 6:12; 1 Pet. 3:13-22). Instead of saying "Caesar is Lord," Christians said that only Christ is Lord.

perseverance (PUR-seh-VEER-ants) means persistence, or keeping on without becoming discouraged. Christians are encouraged by Paul to have perseverance in prayers for their brothers (Eph. 6:18).

Persia (PUR-zha): an empire which dominated Asia from 539 to 331 B.C. Cyrus the Great, a Persian ruler, allowed the Jews to return from Babylonian captivity (2 Chron. 36:22-23), and Darius I allowed them to begin rebuilding the Temple (Ezra 6).

Peter (PEE-ter), who is also called Simon Peter, was perhaps the most prominent of the twelve apostles in the gospels. Jesus gave him the name Peter, which means "rock" (John 1:42). He was outspoken and quick-tempered, a devoted follower of Jesus. It was Peter who preached the first sermon in Jerusalem on Pentecost day (Acts 2:14-36).

The New Testament contains two of Peter's letters (see "Letters," p. 23). The first of these shows that Peter placed particular importance on the suffering of Christians (1 Pet. 3:13-22; see also ch. 6).

Pharaoh (FAY-roh) was the title of ancient Egyptian rulers. Moses was raised in Pharaoh's courts as a child, and he later forced the Pharaoh to allow God's people to go into the promised land of Canaan (see EXODUS; and "The Exodus," p. 34).

Pharisees (FAIR-ih-seez): one of the main divisions of Jews during New Testament times. The Pharisees, who strongly emphasized obedience to God, were the most influential with the people. In the New Testament, they often appear among Jesus' opponents because of their intolerance of others and their tendency to emphasize external matters to the neglect of more important things (Matt. 23; see SADDUCEES).

Philemon (fih-LEE-mun) was a Christian in Colossae, apparently converted by the apostle Paul. The little New Testament letter named Philemon is addressed to him (see p. 26; and ONESIMUS).

Philip (FIL-ip) is the name of two important men in the New Testament. One was an apostle and a friend of Andrew and Peter who came from the same fishing village. He may have first been a follower of John the Baptist. It was Philip who brought Nathanael to Jesus (John 1:43-48).

The other man named Philip is sometimes confused with the apostle named Philip. He was a Greek-speaking Jew, one of the seven men appointed to serve the Jerusalem church (Acts 6:1-6). In Acts 8, we read of his preaching first in Samaria and then on the road to Gaza. In Acts 21 Philip was living in Caesarea and had four unmarried daughters who prophesied.

Philippi (fih-LIP-eye or FIL-ih-pie) was a city in the northeastern part of what is now Greece (see maps F, G). It was named after Philip of Macedonia, Alexander the Great's father, some three-and-a-half centuries before Christ. Philippi was the first city of Europe visited by the apostle Paul. There he was imprisoned and then miraculously released (Acts 16). The New Testament contains a letter to the church in this city.

Philippians (See p. 25.)

Philistines (fih-LIS-teenz or FIL-is-teenz): a people who lived along the coastal areas of Canaan during much of the Old Testament period. They were generally enemies of Israel and an immoral people. It was in battle with the Philistines that David killed the giant Goliath (1 Sam. 17).

Phoebe (FEE-bee) was a deaconess in the church at Cenchreae and was apparently entrusted to carry Paul's letter to Rome (Rom. 16:1-2).

Phoenicia (feh-NISH-uh) was a country along the eastern Mediterranean coast about 120 miles long (see maps C and E). Tyre and Sidon were among the most famous of the Phoenician cities. One of the Phoenician kings, Hiram, was friendly with both David and Solomon and helped in the building of the Jerusalem Temple (1 Kings 7:13-47). The religion of the Phoenicians, however, was pagan (1 Kings 16:31; 18:19).

Pilate (PIE-l't) was the representative of the Roman government in Palestine at the time of Christ. The gospels tell how Pilate thought Jesus to be innocent of the charges made against him but allowed him to be executed anyway. He simply said, "I wash my hands of the deed" (John 18:28–19:16). Tradition tells us that Pilate eventually took his own life.

Pisidia (pih-SID-ee-uh) was a small Roman province in southern Asia Minor. Paul visited the city of Antioch in Pisidia twice (Acts 13:14-50; 14:21-24).

plagues (PLAYGZ) are terrible hardships or difficulties. In the Bible, the word usually refers to the events just before the exodus. When Moses asked the Egyptian Pharaoh to let Israel leave Egypt, Pharaoh refused. In order to force Pharaoh to allow Israel to leave, Moses brought ten plagues upon Egypt. In order, they consisted of (1) water turning to blood, (2) frogs, (3) lice, (4) flies, (5) sickness of cattle, (6) boils on men and animals, (7) hail, (8) locusts, (9) darkness, and (10) death of the firstborn. After these ten plagues, Pharaoh allowed the Israelites to leave Egypt (Exod. 7–12).

poetry is a type of writing that is more rhythmical or musical than ordinary writing and expresses more feeling. The Bible contains some great poetry (see p. 15).

Potiphar (POT-ih-fer) was one of Pharaoh's officers who bought Joseph as his slave and then raised him to a trusted place in his household (Gen. 39:1-20).

Potter's Field was a piece of ground which the priests bought with the money Judas received for betraying Jesus. It was used by the Jews to bury strangers who died in Jerusalem (Matt. 27:7; Acts 1:18).

praise (PRAYZ) means words or deeds which give honor or glory to their object. The book of Psalms contains a great deal of praise to God.

prayer (See p. 96.)

priest (PREEST) in the Old Testament meant a special person who served as a go-between for God and the people. The priests wore special clothes, offered sacrifices, and prayed on behalf of the people (Lev. 4; 16; Num. 3).

The New Testament teaches that Christ is the perfect High Priest, bringing men together with God in a special manner (Heb. 6:20; 7:1-17). Because of this, Christians are all priests and no longer depend on special men to pray for them, although Christians do pray for one another (Eph. 2:18; 1 Pet. 2:5, 9).

Prisca or **Priscilla** (PRIS-kuh or prih-SIL-uh) was the wife of a Jewish Christian named Aquila. Prisca and Aquila were tentmakers and friends of Paul (Acts 18:2). They taught Apollos in Ephesus where they had a house in which the church met and worshiped (Acts 18:24-26; 1 Cor. 16:19).

Prison Epistles (See p. 23.)

proconsul (PRO-kon-s'l) was the title of a rank of Roman officials who served as deputy consuls in Roman provinces (Acts 13:7; 18:12).

procurator (PRAH-kyoo-RAY-ter) was the title of a governor of a Roman province. These men were usually appointed by the emperor himself. Pilate, Felix, and Festus were procurators (Luke 3:1; Acts 23:26; 24:27).

promise (PROM-is): usually, in the Bible, God's intention to bless and redeem his people. Christ was the fulfillment of God's promises through Abraham, David, and the prophets (2 Cor. 1:20; Eph. 3:6).

prophecy (PRAH-feh-see) is the word of God delivered by chosen men (prophets). There are many books of prophecy in the Old Testament (see p. 16). The New Testament book of prophecy is Revelation (see p. 27).

prophet (PRAH-fet): one who spoke for God as God directed. Often the messages of the prophets were words of judgment and criticism against the sins of God's people. Sometimes they foretold events in the future. Some of the most important of the Old Testament prophets are Isaiah, Jeremiah, Ezekiel, and Hosea.

proselyte (PRAHS-uh-lite): a Gentile convert to Judaism (Acts 2:10; 6:5).

proverbs (PRAH-vurbz) are short sayings which may take the form of questions or comparisons. The Old Testament book of Proverbs is an entire book of such sayings (see p. 15).

providence (PRAHV-ih-dents): God's continuing care and rule over the entire creation (Ps. 104:10-25; Matt. 4:4; Acts 17:25-28).

psalms (SALMZ) are songs or poems, usually containing praise. The Old Testament book of Psalms contains 150 such works, written by David, Solomon, and others (see p. 15).

publican (PUB-lih-kun): a tax collector for the Roman government. Such men were hated by the Jews because they worked for the despised foreign government which ruled them. Matthew and Zacchaeus were publicans (Matt. 9:11; 21:31; Luke 19:2).

Purim, Feast of (PYOOR-im): a feast which celebrated the deliverance of the Jews by Esther from destruction by the king of Persia (Esth. 9:1-10).

pyramids (PEER-uh-midz): the great tombs of the Egyptian

Pharaohs. The ruins of over eighty of these ancient monuments still exist.

Q

quail (KWAYL): a bird which God provided as food for the Israelites when they were wandering in the wilderness of Zin (Exod. 16:13).

R

rabbi (RAB-eye) is a Jewish title which means master or teacher. Jesus' disciples called him "Rabbi" (Matt. 23:7-8; John 1:38; 6:25).

Rachel (RAY-ch'l) was the wife of Jacob, the mother of Joseph and Benjamin. She died as Benjamin was born (Gen. 29:6, 16, 18, 31; 30:1-8).

Rahab (RAY-hab) was a woman who lived in Jericho and played an important part in its conquest by the Israelites. She hid the Israelite spies who came into Jericho before the city was attacked. Because of her help, her house and family were spared (Josh. 2–6).

Rebecca or **Rebekah** (reh-BEK-uh) was the sister of Laban and the wife of Isaac. She was the mother of Isaac's two sons, Jacob and Esau (Gen. 22:20-24; 24, 25).

reconciliation (REK-un-sil-ee-AY-shun): in the Bible, the restoring or rebuilding of man's relationship with God which has been broken or damaged by man's sin. Basically, reconciliation is something that God does for man, rather than something that man does for himself. God reconciles us through Jesus' life and teaching, death on the cross, and resurrection. Men who are reconciled to God are also reconciled to each other. One of the important purposes of the church is to tell and show the world the good news of God's reconciliation (2 Cor. 5:18).

redemption (ree-DEMP-shun) comes from a term of the marketplace meaning "to buy back." To the Christian, it means the act of God in delivering man from sin through Jesus Christ (Rom. 3:24; 1 Cor. 6:20). In so doing, God sets man free from the bondage of sin (Rom. 6:4).

Red Sea: a 1,350 mile-long gulf which joins the Mediterranean Sea with the Indian Ocean (see map D). It was across a small arm of the Red Sea that God miraculously delivered Israel from Egyptian captivity (Exod. 13:17-18).

Rehoboam (RE-ho-BO-um) was the son of King Solomon and followed him on the throne of Israel. He began to reign over Israel when he was about forty-one years old (1 Kings 11:43). He was an unwise ruler, listening to his younger advisors and rejecting the wisdom of the older men. He took heavy taxes from the people and refused to lighten them. During his reign Israel was divided into two kingdoms (1 Kings 12–14).

remnant (REM-nunt) is a term often used to describe those who survive a war, battle, or period of captivity. Israel's prophets looked forward to a remnant through whom God would build a new people (Isa. 10:20-23).

repentance (ree-PEN-tants) is feeling sorry for having done wrong, and turning away from such wrongdoing. Many people think of repentance only as sorrow. True repentance, however, also involves an active turning away from wrong and toward God. In order to accept God's love in Christ and his forgiveness and reconciliation, we must repent and turn to God (Matt. 3:2; 4:17; Acts 2:38; 20:21; 2 Pet. 3:9).

resurrection (REZ-uh-REC-shun) (See pp. 47 and 96.)

Reuben (ROO-ben) was the oldest son of Jacob and Leah. It was Reuben who talked his brothers into selling Joseph as a slave rather than taking his life (Gen. 37:19-22). As one of Jacob's twelve sons, Reuben was the father of one of Israel's twelve tribes, the Reubenites (Gen. 29:32; see map B).

revelation (REV-uh-LAY-shun) refers to the way God makes himself known to man. In the Old Testament, God revealed himself to his people through different events and special men like Abraham, Moses, and the prophets. The New Testament contains God's fullest revelation of himself through his Son, Jesus Christ (Heb. 1:1-3; see "Knowledge through God's Word," p. 63).

Revelation is also the name of the last book of the New Testament, also called the Revelation to John.

Roman Empire (RO-mun EM-pire): the empire headquartered in Rome and beginning in 31 B.C. It included all of Italy for some time and finally extended over the whole Mediterranean world, present-day France, Britain, and Germany. It lasted until the fifth century A.D., when moral corruption within and the growing strength of its enemies led to its collapse. It was

this empire which ruled Palestine in the time of Christ and from which the Jewish people longed for deliverance. It was also the Roman Empire which persecuted the early church (Acts 8:1).

Rome: the capital of the great Roman Empire, and of modern Italy. It lies on the west coast of Italy about seventeen miles from the mouth of the Tiber River (see maps F, G). The city was founded perhaps as early as 1000 B.C. During the time of Christ, the population of the city was over 1,000,000 and may have been as high as 4,000,000. More than half the population was made up of slaves.

Ruth was a Moabite woman who married an Israelite and was soon widowed. Ruth and her mother-in-law, Naomi, returned to Israel. The book of Ruth tells the story of how she then married a second husband, Boaz (see p. 14).

S

sabachthani (suh-BAHK-thuh-nee) is an Aramaic word which Jesus used while on the cross when he said, "My God, my God, why hast thou forsaken me?" (Matt. 27:46; Mark 15:34). It has been suggested that he was quoting Psalm 22:1.

Sabbath (SAB-uth) means "cease" or "rest" and was the name of the Jewish day of rest, the seventh day. Genesis tells us that God rested on the seventh day of creation (Gen. 2:3). Israel held special worship services on the sabbath day and observed special practices in honor of God's creation and the past acts of deliverance (Exod. 16:22-30; Deut. 5:15).

sackcloth (SAK-kloth) is a coarse material of dark color, often made of goat's hair. It was worn by mourners, prophets, and captives (2 Sam. 3:31; 1 Kings 20:31; Isa. 20:2).

sacrifice (SAK-rih-fice) is a religious act through which God is honored by a gift (Gen. 12:7; Lev. 4:1-35; Num. 7:1-11). God does not need material gifts, but Old Testament sacrifices were important as a symbol of the worshiper's dedication of himself. This sacrifice or gift of one's self, not an animal sacrifice, is what the new covenant requires (Rom. 12:1-2).

Sadducees (SAD-you-seez): one of the main divisions in first-century Judaism (with the Pharisees, Zealots, and Essenes). They were a relatively small group but were very influential and held many high offices. They were frequent opponents of Jesus (Matt. 16:6, 11-12; 22:23; Mark 12:18; Luke 19:47).

saint: one of God's people. The word basically means one who has been set aside for a special purpose in God's plan, but in the New Testament, it simply refers to a Christian (2 Chron. 6:41; Ps. 16:3; Acts 9:13; 1 Cor. 16:1; Eph. 4:12).

Salome (suh-LO-mee) was a popular name in Bible times. Two women by that name are particularly important. First, there was Salome who was the mother of Jesus' disciples, James and John. She was present at Jesus' crucifixion and was one of the women who came to the tomb and discovered that the resurrection had occurred (Mark 16:1).

Second, there was the wicked daughter of Herodias, who danced before Herod and pleased him so much that he offered her a reward. She chose to have John the Baptist killed (Mark 6:17-28).

Salt Sea (See DEAD SEA.)

salvation (sal-VAY-shun) can mean deliverance from any type of evil. But the Christian understands salvation as the process by which man is freed from sin and given the blessings of God (Matt. 1:21; Rom. 6; 2 Cor. 7:10; Eph. 1:13).

Samaria (suh-MAIR-ee-uh) was another name for the Northern Kingdom after Israel became divided into two realms (see "Kingdom and Exile," p. 36). In the time of Christ, Samaria was still one of the divisions of Palestine (see map E). It was the home of the Samaritans, who were held in contempt by the Jews (John 8:48). Jesus, however, used one of these hated Samaritans as one of the most favorable characters in his parables (Luke 10:25-37; see also 1 Kings 16:24).

Samson (SAM-sun) was one of the judges of Israel, possibly the last judge before Samuel and the beginning of the kingdom. He is remembered for his great strength, short temper, and lack of wisdom (Judg. 13–16). He died after being captured and tortured by the Philistines, pulling down the pillars of an idol's temple and destroying many of his enemies with himself.

Samuel (SAM-you-el) was the last of Israel's judges and an early prophet (1 Sam. 3:20; 7:15-17). When Samuel was born, his mother Hannah took him to the priest Eli and dedicated him to God's service (1 Sam. 1:24-28). In his later years, Samuel anointed both Saul and David to the office of king of Israel (1 Sam. 10; 16). Samuel is an important figure in the books of the Old Testament which bear his name (see "History," pp. 13-14).

sanctify (SANK-tih-fie) means to set apart and dedicate to God. In the Old Testament, sanctification referred to any people, objects, or seasons used for worship (Exod. 13:2; Lev. 27:14, 16; Neh. 13:19-22, KJV). In the New Testament, it refers to what occurs in the lives of all Christians when the Holy Spirit comes to dwell in them at the time of their baptism (Eph. 5:26; Heb. 13:12).

Sanhedrin (san-HEE-drin): the highest Jewish governing body during the Greek and Roman periods. The Sanhedrin council had seventy members plus the high priest, who presided over its functions (Acts 4:5-18).

Sapphira (suh-FIE-ruh) was the wife of Ananias. They were members of the early church in Jerusalem. They lied to God about a gift they were bringing, and were struck dead (Acts 5:1-10).

Sarah (sometimes spelled Sara) was the wife of Abraham and the mother of Isaac. Her name was originally Sarai, but God changed it just as he changed Abram's to Abraham. She was Abraham's wife for many years before Isaac was born (Gen. 17:15-27). She is called the mother of the Hebrew race (Isa. 51:1-2).

Satan (SAY-tun): the name given to the enemy of both God and man. He is also called the devil, Lucifer, Belial, or Beelzebub. The Bible teaches that he continually seeks to defeat God's purposes but will ultimately be destroyed (1 Pet. 5:8; Rev. 20:10).

Saul (SAWL) was the first king of Israel. He was anointed by Samuel and began as a good king (1 Sam. 11–14). Later, however, he became unfaithful to God and jealous of David.

He ended his own life after being wounded in a battle (see 1 Sam. 16–31; and "Kingdom and Exile," p. 36).

Saul is also the Hebrew name of the apostle Paul (see Acts 13:9).

Savior (SAVE-yor): one who saves or delivers others from any danger or evil. In the Old Testament, God is thought of as the Savior because of his many acts of deliverance on behalf of his people (Ps. 44:3, 7; Isa. 43:11). In the New Testament, Jesus is shown to be the Savior because of his saving life, death, and resurrection, which delivers us from evil and death (Luke 2:11; Titus 1:4; 2 Pet. 1:1; 2:20; 1 John 4:14).

scapegoat (SKAPE-gote): a goat that was used on the Jews' yearly Day of Atonement. The priests prayed over it, transferring the people's sins onto it, and then it was released in the wilderness (Lev. 16:8, 10, 20-22).

Sceva (SEE-vuh) was a Jew living in Ephesus who had seven sons who were magicians. They tried to use Jesus' name to perform mighty works and were themselves publicly embarrassed (Acts 19:14-17).

scribes were a class of men in Judaism who studied the Jewish Law and devoted themselves to preserving and copying the Law. They served as judges and teachers in Jesus' time and were often among his enemies (Matt. 23; Mark 2:16).

scroll (SKROLE): ancient books made of papyrus or animal skins. They did not have pages but were rolled on two sticks. Some scrolls were as long as thirty-five feet (Isa. 34:4; Jer. 36; Rev. 5; 10:1-10).

Sea of Galilee (See GALILEE, SEA OF.)

second coming: the return of Christ which he told his apostles about shortly before his crucifixion (John 14:3). The writers of the letters in the New Testament often refer to this event as the "blessed hope" that Christ will return to claim those who honor him as Lord (Rom. 8:18-27; 1 Cor. 15:22-28; Eph. 1:14; Titus 2:13).

Semites (SEM-ites) is a term that comes from the name *Shem*, who was Noah's son. It refers to a large group of ancient peoples who descended from Shem. They lived in the area surrounding the Tigris and Euphrates rivers (Gen. 10:21-31). The Jews and the Arabs are the largest groups of Semites in the modern world.

Septuagint (SEP-too-uh-jint): the first and most important translation of the Old Testament from Hebrew into Greek. The translation was completed some time in the third century before Christ. The name "Septuagint" comes from the Greek word for "seventy" because the translation was traditionally supposed to have been made by seventy men. The translation was made in Alexandria, Egypt, where there were many Jews who spoke Greek.

sepulchre (SEP-ul-ker): another word for tomb.

Sergius Paulus (See PAULUS, SERGIUS.)

Seth was Adam's third son (Gen. 4:25; 5:3-8).

Shechem (SHE-kem): a city in the hill country of the tribal area of Ephraim, between Mount Ebal and Mount Gerizim (see maps A, B, C). Jacob owned land there (Gen. 33:18-20), and his son Joseph was buried there (Josh. 24:32).

Shem was the second son of Noah and the founder of the Semitic race (Gen. 11:10).

Sheol (SHE-ohl) is the Old Testament word for what is called in the New Testament "Hades." It is the place of the dead (Luke 16:19-31).

Sidon (SIGH-d'n) was a city of Phoenicia (see maps A-G), an important port and trade center. Idolatry was common there (Isa. 23; Ezek. 28; Matt. 11:21-22). Jesus visited there, and some disciples lived there (Matt. 15:21; Mark 7:24-31; Luke 6:17).

Silas (SIGH-lus) was a member of the Jerusalem church and a Roman citizen. He traveled with Paul and Barnabas from Jerusalem to Antioch (Acts 15:22-32). He also accompanied Paul on his missionary journeys and was among Paul's closest and most trusted helpers (see Acts 16–18). Some of Paul's letters (1 and 2 Thess.) were apparently written by Silas, also called Silvanus, who acted as Paul's secretary.  It is almost certain that the man named Silvanus who acted as Peter's secretary in writing 1 Peter is the same person (1 Pet. 5:12).

Siloam (sih-LOW-um) was a reservoir of water in Jerusalem. Jesus sent a blind man to wash there, and he was healed (John 9:7).

Simeon (SIM-ee-un) is the name of several Bible characters. One was the second son of Jacob and the father of the tribe of Simeon (Gen. 29:33; see map B). A second Simeon was a devout Jew who praised God when he held the infant Jesus (Luke 2:25-35).

Simon (SIGH-mun) is a common Bible name. Simon Peter

was the brother of Andrew, a disciple and an apostle (see PETER). Another of the twelve apostles of Jesus was called Simon the Cananaean, who was a member of the Jewish party called Zealots (Matt. 10:4).

There was also Simon the leper (Matt. 26:6); Simon of Cyrene, who was forced by the Romans to help carry Jesus' cross (Matt. 27:32); and Simon Magus, a magician of Samaria who tried to buy the Holy Spirit (Acts 8:9-13) and was rebuked by Peter (Acts 8:14-24).

sin (See pp. 76-77.)

Sinai (SIGH-nigh) is a name given to both a mountain and a broader area of land. Mount Sinai is the mountain on which God met and talked with Moses, giving him the Law (Exod. 19). Its exact location is uncertain. The peninsula north of the Red Sea and east of Egypt is called the Sinai peninsula (see map D).

Sodom (SOD-um) was one of the cities which God destroyed because of its wickedness. Abraham's nephew, Lot, lived there (Gen. 19). It was located somewhere near the south end of the Dead Sea, and water probably covers the area now (see map A).

Solomon (SAHL-oh-mun) was the third and last king of the undivided Israel. He was the son of David and Bathsheba. For most of his reign, he was a good ruler, especially known for his wisdom. Israel became prosperous and famous under his rule (1 Kings 6; 2 Chron. 1-9). He built the Temple in Jerusalem and is thought to have written the books of Proverbs, Song of Solomon, Ecclesiastes, and at least two of the Psalms (Pss. 72, 127; see "Kingdom and Exile," p. 36).

Son of God is a frequent New Testament title for Jesus Christ (John 3:18; 10:36; Acts 9:20; Rom. 1:4; see also "The Coming of Jesus," p. 41).

Son of Man is a title Jesus sometimes used for himself, indicating both the fact that he was a man and the fact that he would be triumphant and victorious among men (Dan. 7:13-14; Matt. 8:20; 9:6; 12:8).

Song of Solomon (See p. 16.)

soul is a word often used in the Bible for the part of man which is not material or body (Matt. 10:28).

spirit is sometimes used to mean the same as soul in the Bible. Man's spirit is often spoken of as that part of him through which he has a direct relationship with God (John 4:23-24; 1 Cor. 6:17).

Spirit, Holy (See HOLY SPIRIT.)

spiritual gifts are special gifts given by the Holy Spirit to some Christians for the service of the church. Several lists of these gifts are given in the New Testament (Rom. 12:6-8; 1 Cor. 12:4-11, 28-30). Examples of spiritual gifts are teaching, giving, and preaching.

Stephen (STEE-ven) was one of seven men appointed to serve the Jerusalem church (Acts 6:1-6).  The seventh chapter of Acts tells how Stephen's preaching offended many of the Jews. Because of his preaching, Stephen was stoned to death and became the first Christian martyr (Acts 7:57-60).

stewardship (STOO-erd-ship) is the responsibility of managing what belongs to another. Christians regard themselves as stewards of God's creation and all they own in this life (1 Pet. 4:10; see also p. 31).

stoning was an ordinary form of punishment in Hebrew Law (Lev. 24:16; Deut. 13:6-10). Stephen was stoned (Acts 7:58-60), and Paul's enemies once tried to stone him (Acts 14:19).

Supper, Lord's (See LORD'S SUPPER.)

synagogue (SIN-uh-gog) was a place where Jews came together to read and study the Old Testament. The term refers both to the people organized into a religious community and to the place where they came together. Although there was only one Temple in Jerusalem, there were many synagogues throughout the Mediterranean world (Matt. 4:23; Luke 4:16-17; Acts 13:15).

synoptic (sin-OP-tik) means "seeing together." The first three gospels, Matthew, Mark, and Luke, are often called the synoptic gospels because they contain most of the same incidents in Jesus' life and have a similar view of his ministry. (See also "Gospels," pp. 21-22.)

Syria (SEER-ee-uh) was a shortened form of "Assyria." It lies east of the Mediterranean Sea, north of Galilee, and northwest of the Arabian desert (see map D).

T

tabernacle (TAB-er-nak-'l) means "tent." It usually refers to Israel's movable place of worship. It was taken with them during the period of wandering in the wilderness, then moved from place to place during the period of judges

(Num. 7:89). King David had it brought to Jerusalem, and later, under Solomon, it was replaced by the Temple.

The tabernacle was made of cloth drapes, animal skins, and wooden supports. It was about forty-five feet long and fifteen feet wide. It had  two rooms which were separated by a heavy curtain. One of these rooms, called the holy place, contained an incense altar, golden candlesticks, and the table of showbread. The other room was called the holy of holies and could be entered only by the high priest. It contained the ark of the covenant, a small boxlike container made of wood and covered with gold. The ark contained the tablets of Law, manna, and Aaron's rod (Exod. 25:10–27:19).

Tabernacles, Feast of: One of Israel's sacred feasts, also called the Feast of Booths, celebrating the entrance into the promised land (Lev. 23:34; Deut. 16:13).

Tabitha (TAB-ih-thuh): a Christian woman who lived in Joppa and made clothes to give to poor widows. When she died, the apostle Peter was sent for, and he raised her from the dead (Acts 9:36-43).

Talmud (TAL-mud): a collection of Jewish teachings and traditions which were written down during the early Christian period.

Tarsus (TAR-sus) was the birthplace and early home of the apostle Paul. It was an ancient city, ten miles inland from the Mediterranean in the province of Cilicia (see maps F, G).

taxes, when mentioned in the Bible, may be political—set by the government—or ecclesiastical—set by the religious authorities. The Hebrews paid taxes after the years of wandering were over (Exod. 30:13). In New Testament times, the Romans collected taxes in Palestine (Matt. 17:24; 22:17).

temple (TEM-p'l): a place of worship. King Solomon built Israel's first Temple, replacing the tabernacle. Solomon's Temple had three parts: a porch through which one entered the Temple; a holy place which was sixty feet long, thirty feet wide, and forty-five feet high; and a holy of holies which was thirty feet long, high, and wide (1 Kings 7). Solomon's Temple was destroyed by the Babylonians (2 Kings 25:8-17). After this, a Temple was rebuilt by Zerubbabel (Ezra 3–6), and later, by Herod the Great. Herod's Temple was destroyed in A.D. 70 when the Roman army destroyed Jerusalem.

temptation (temp-TAY-shun): the attraction which wrongdoing has or seems to have. Because of the way in which temptation is a sort of contest, some temptations may be seen as tests in which one gains strength to do right (Heb. 12:4-11; 1 Pet. 1:7; 4:12, 13). But this does not mean that one should set out to tempt himself, for temptation should be avoided if possible (Gal. 6:1).

Ten Commandments (See COMMANDMENTS.)

Teraphim (TEHR-uh-fim) are small statues or idols which many ancient people worshiped as false gods (Gen. 31:19; 1 Sam. 19:13-16; see also p. 84).

testament (TES-tuh-ment) means a covenant or agreement (see OLD TESTAMENT and NEW TESTAMENT; and "Covenant," p. 91).

Thaddaeus (THAD-dee-us) was one of the twelve apostles (Matt. 10:3; Mark 3:18) about whom nothing else is known.

Theophilus (thee-OF-ih-lus) is the person to whom Luke wrote the New Testament books of Luke and Acts (Luke 1:3; Acts 1:1). He was probably a Christian of some official rank in the Roman government.

Thessalonians, 1 and 2 (See p. 25.)

Thessalonica (THES-uh-low-NIE-kuh) was one of the most important cities in Macedonia, the country which was the home of the famous Alexander the Great (see maps F, G). Its ancient name was Therma, but in 315 B.C. it was renamed Thessalonica for the sister of Alexander the Great. When the apostle Paul obeyed the "Macedonian call" (Acts 16:9), the first major city that he visited was Philippi. From there he and Silas (and perhaps Timothy) went 100 miles west to Thessalonica, where they established a church (Acts 17:1-9). The New Testament contains two of Paul's letters to these Christians (see p. 25).

Thomas (TOM-us) was one of the twelve apostles (Matt. 10:3). He was also called Didymus or "the Twin" (John 11:16; 20:24; 21:2). Thomas is often remembered because of his refusal to believe that Jesus was really raised from the grave until he actually saw his scars (John 20:24-29). But he is also the apostle who, shortly before the crucifixion, said "Let us also go, that we may die with him" (John 11:16).

Thummim (See URIM AND THUMMIM.)

Tiberius (tie-BEER-ee-us) was the name of the Roman emperor or Caesar at the time of Jesus' death. It was also another name for the Sea of Galilee. Tiberius died in A.D. 37.

Tigris (TIE-gris) was one of the two great rivers of Mesopotamia. It begins in the Taurus mountains and flows some 1,150 miles to the Persian gulf (see map D). The prophet Daniel was standing on the banks of the Tigris when he had his great vision (Dan. 10:4).

Timothy (TIM-oh-thee) was the son of a Gentile father and a Jewish mother. He became a close friend and companion of the apostle Paul and often served as his representative (Phil. 2:19-22; 1 Tim. 1:2; 2 Tim. 4:9). Two of the letters in the New Testament are from the apostle Paul to Timothy (see pp. 24-26).

tithe (TIETH) is a tenth of one's income set aside for special use. The Law of Moses required that one-tenth of all crops, land, and livestock should be given to the support of the priesthood (Lev. 27:30-33).

Titus (TIE-tus) was one of the apostle Paul's converts. He was a trusted friend and helper in the apostle's work (2 Cor. 2:13; 7:5-16; Titus 1:4). Paul's letter to Titus is found in the New Testament (see pp. 24, 26).

tomb (TOOM) means a place of burial. In Bible times, tombs were of different kinds. Some were under the ground, but others were dug into stone cliffs or built as small buildings above the ground. Often large stones weighing several tons were rolled over the door of tombs. Jesus was buried in such a tomb and an angel rolled the stone away (Luke 24:2; John 20:1).

Torah (TOW-ruh) is the Hebrew word for "law." It became a common name for the first five books of the Old Testament.

transfiguration (tranz-FIG-you-RAY-shun): the event in

Jesus' ministry when he changed his appearance in front of Peter, James, and John (Mark 9:2-3; Matt. 17:2).

transgression (tranz-GREH-shun) means the breaking of a law (Prov. 17:19; Rom. 4:15). It is sometimes used to mean sin (see "Sin," pp. 76 and 97).

translate (TRANS-late) usually means to change from one language into another. The Bible has been translated from the original Hebrew, Aramaic, and Greek into many languages (see ch. 1). The word can also mean to change from one place or state to another. In this way, Christians have been "translated" from darkness into the kingdom of God's Son (Col. 1:13).

tribes are groups of people all descended from the same ancestor. The twelve tribes of the Hebrew nation all descended from the twelve sons of Jacob, grandson of Abraham (Gen. 49:11-28; see map B). Jacob's twelve sons were Reuben, Simeon, Levi, Judah, Zebulun, Issachar, Dan, Gad, Asher, Naphtali, Joseph (who later became father of two tribes through his sons Ephraim and Manasseh), and Benjamin.

During the time of the Old Testament some of the tribes merged, and grew in importance, and others became less important (Num. 2:3; 32:33; 1 Chron. 27:16-22; 1 Kings 12:20). After both the northern and southern kingdoms went into captivity, the identities of the tribes were lost so that they were never again mentioned in the historical writings by name.

Troas (TROW-az) was one of the most important cities in northwest Asia. It was a Roman colony located ten miles from the ruins of the ancient city of Troy on the Aegean Sea (see maps F, G). It was in Troas that Paul had a vision which led him to take Christ's message to Europe (Acts 16:8-9).

Trumpets, Feast of: a celebration that began the Jewish civil year (Lev. 23:23-24).

Tychicus (TIK-ih-kus) was an Asian Christian and helper to the apostle Paul, whom Paul trusted to do important tasks. Tychicus carried Paul's letters to the Colossians and Ephesians (Col. 4:7-9; Eph. 6:21).

Tyre (TIRE) was a Phoenician coastal city south of Sidon and north of Mount Carmel (see maps A-G). Both Jesus (Mark 7:24-31) and Paul (Acts 21:3-7) visited this area.

U

unleavened bread (un-LEV-end) was made without leavening, or any substance to make it rise, and eaten at the Jewish Feast of Passover (Exod. 12:8). Christians today eat unleavened bread when they eat the Lord's Supper, since it was when Jesus was eating the Passover that he told his disciples to eat the bread in his memory (Matt. 26:26-29; Mark 14:22-25).

Unleavened Bread, Feast of. (See PASSOVER.)

Uriah (you-RYE-uh) was a Hittite who served in David's army. He was the husband of Bathsheba. David sinned in causing Uriah's death in order that he might take Bathsheba as his own wife (2 Sam. 11).

Urim and Thummim (YOU-rim and THUM-im) were objects, perhaps stones, which were carried in the Jewish high priest's breastplate. They were used in determining the will of God in important matters (Exod. 28:30).

Uzziah (uh-ZIE-uh) was the eleventh king of Judah. He was also called Azariah. During the fifty-two years of his reign, he strengthened the kingdom and showed great ability. But he also drifted away from the Lord and suffered because of this (2 Kings 14:22; 2 Chron. 26:1-10; 16-21).

V

vengeance (VEN-jents) is a type of punishment intended to make up for a wrong already done, or "get back" at the wrongdoer (Judg. 15:7; Jer. 11:20; Rom. 12:19).

versions (VER-zhunz) are different translations of scripture (see ch. 1).

vow: a solemn promise to God, usually accompanied by some outward sign (Gen. 28:20-22; Judg. 11:30-31).

W

wave offering: a type of sacrifice in the Old Testament in which the priest would wave the offering back and forth (Exod. 29:24-28).

Way, the: One of the earliest names given for Christians (Acts 9:2; 19:9; 22:4; see also "The Church as a New Community," p. 52).

Weeks, Feast of. (See PENTECOST.)

Wilderness of Zin: a desert southwest of the Dead Sea, near the borders of Canaan (Num. 13:21; see map A). After God led the Israelites out of Egypt, they became unfaithful, and because of this he caused them to wander in the wilderness of Zin for forty years before reaching the promised land (Num. 14:33; 32:13). During this period, the Hebrew people had to learn to depend upon God, and he provided them with daily food (see MANNA; QUAIL).

Word of God: a term usually referring either to Christ (who is God's Word; see John 1:1) or to the inspired writings of the Bible. Often these two different meanings are made clear by simply capitalizing the letter "W" when Christ is meant (see "The Coming of Jesus," p. 41).

worship (See p. 97.)

wrath (RATH): anger. In the Bible, it is often used to refer to God's attitude toward sin and evil (Rom. 1:18; Eph. 5:6), though he continues to love the sinners (Rom. 5:8; 1 Tim. 1:15).

X

Xerxes (ZURK-seez) was the king of Persia from 486 to 465 B.C. He was also called Ahasuerus and is mentioned in the Old Testament books of Ezra (4:6), Esther (1:1, etc.), and Daniel (9:1).

Y

Yahweh (YAH-way): a name for God. Its history is interesting and a bit difficult to understand. Because they wanted to honor God, the Jews refused to say or even write his name. So they only wrote the consonants, as we might write "JMS" for "James." After many years of writing it this way and never pronouncing it, no one remembered the vowels.

Only the consonants YHWH remained. Many centuries later, the vowels from the Hebrew word for "Lord" were added, making the name something like "Jehovah." Most scholars agree that the original name must have sounded more like "Yahweh."

yoke: a wooden bar which is tied around the neck of farm animals (Num. 19:2). Sometimes the word is used, however, to refer to a pair of oxen (1 Sam. 14:4, KJV). And the word is also used symbolically, as when Jesus speaks of the yoke of his teaching as one that is light (Matt. 11:29-30; also Isa. 9:4).

Z

Zacchaeus (za-KEE-us) was a publican or tax collector for the Roman government who lived in Jericho. When he became a disciple of Jesus, his life was greatly changed (Luke 19:1-8).

Zacharias (ZAK-uh-RYE-us) was a priest, the father of John the Baptist. When he doubted an angel who told him that he was to have a son, he was stricken dumb until the child was born and given the name John (Luke 1).

Zealots (ZEL-uts): one of the major Jewish parties or divisions in the time of Christ. They were dedicated to resisting the aggressions and the rule of the Roman government. One of Jesus' apostles, Simon the Cananaean, was a member of this group (Luke 6:15; Acts 1:13).

Zebedee (ZEB-uh-dee) was a fisherman on the Sea of Galilee who had two sons, James and John, who became apostles of Jesus (Mark 1:19-20).

Zebulun (ZEB-you-lun) was a son of Jacob and Leah (Gen. 30:19-20) and thus head of one of the tribes of Israel (Num. 1:31; see map B).

Zechariah (ZEK-uh-RYE-uh) is a form of the name of the father of John the Baptist (see ZACHARIAS).

Zechariah is also the name of an Old Testament prophet and a book of prophecy (see p. 19).

Zephaniah (See p. 18.)

Zerubbabel (zeh-RUB-uh-bel) was in the line of kingship in the nation of Judah. When Cyrus allowed the Jews to return home from captivity, he appointed Zerubbabel governor (Hag. 2:21). He overcame much opposition to see that the Temple was rebuilt (Ezra 4).

Zin (See WILDERNESS OF ZIN.)

Zion (ZIE-on): originally, one of the hills on which Jerusalem stood. When the ark of the covenant was placed there by David, the hill became sacred. Later the name came to mean all of Jerusalem (2 Sam. 5:6-9; Ps. 48) and even heaven (Heb. 12:22).

Zipporah (ZIH-poh-ruh) was the daughter of Jethro and first wife of Moses (Exod. 2:21).

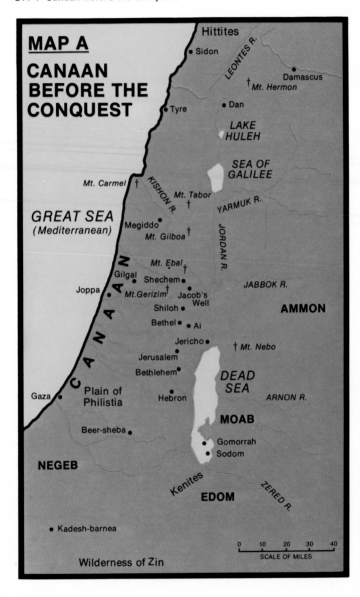

MAP A

CANAAN BEFORE THE CONQUEST

Hittites

• Sidon

LEONTES R.

• Damascus
† Mt. Hermon

• Tyre

• Dan

LAKE HULEH

SEA OF GALILEE

Mt. Carmel †

KISHON R.

† Mt. Tabor

YARMUK R.

GREAT SEA
(Mediterranean)

Megiddo •
Mt. Gilboa †

JORDAN R.

Mt. Ebal †

Gilgal •
Shechem •
Joppa
Mt.Gerizim †
Jacob's Well

JABBOK R.

AMMON

C A N A A N

Shiloh •

Bethel • • Ai

Jericho •

† Mt. Nebo

Jerusalem •

Bethlehem •

DEAD SEA

Gaza •
Plain of Philistia

Hebron •

ARNON R.

MOAB

Beer-sheba •

Gomorrah •
Sodom •

NEGEB

Kenites

ZERED R.

EDOM

• Kadesh-barnea

0 10 20 30 40
SCALE OF MILES

Wilderness of Zin

MAP B
THE TWELVE TRIBES IN CANAAN

- Sidon
- LEONTES R.
- † Mt. Hermon
- Damascus
- **DAN**
- Dan
- Tyre
- **ASHER**
- **NAPHTALI**
- LAKE HULEH
- SEA OF GALILEE
- Mt. Carmel †
- **ZEBU-LUN**
- KISHON R.
- Mt. Tabor
- YARMUK R.
- **ISSA-CHAR**
- JORDAN R.
- **GAD**
- GREAT SEA (Mediterranean)
- Megiddo
- Mt. Gilboa †
- **MANASSEH**
- Samaria
- Gilgal
- † Mt. Ebal
- JABBOK R.
- Joppa
- Mt. Gerizim †
- Shechem
- **EPHRAIM**
- Shiloh
- **GILEAD**
- **AMMON**
- Bethel
- Ai
- **DAN**
- **BENJAMIN**
- Jericho
- † Mt. Nebo
- Jerusalem
- **DEAD SEA**
- **REUBEN**
- Ashkelon
- Bethlehem
- Gaza
- **JUDAH**
- Hebron
- ARNON R.
- Beer-sheba
- **MOAB**
- **SIMEON**
- **EDOM**
- ZERED R.
- Kadesh-barnea

0   10   20   30   40
SCALE OF MILES

MAP C
ISRAEL AND JUDAH

Sidon

LEONTES R.

Damascus

† Mt. Hermon

Tyre

Dan

PHOENICIA

LAKE HULEH

ARAM

SEA OF GALILEE

Mt. Carmel †

KISHON R.

Mt. Tabor †

YARMUK R.

GREAT SEA
(Mediterranean)

Megiddo

SAMARIA

Mt. Gilboa †

JORDAN R.

ISRAEL

Gilgal

Mt. Ebal †

Shechem

JABBOK R.

Joppa

Mt. Gerizim †

Jacob's Well

GILEAD

AMMON

Shiloh

Bethel

Ai

Jericho

† Mt. Nebo

Jerusalem

Bethlehem

PHILISTIA

DEAD SEA

Ashkelon

Tekoa

Hebron

ARNON R.

Gaza

Beer-sheba

Gomorrah

Sodom

MOAB

JUDAH

EDOM

ZERED R.

Kadesh-barnea

0 10 20 30 40

SCALE OF MILES

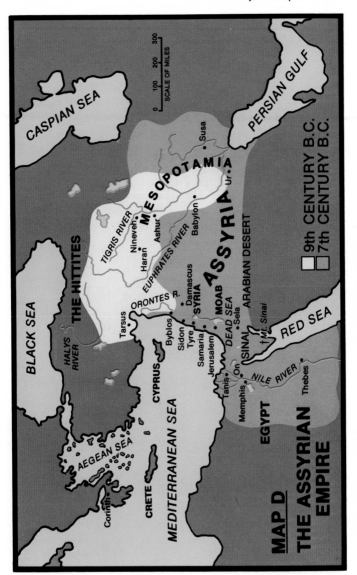

MAP D

THE ASSYRIAN EMPIRE

□ 9th CENTURY B.C.
□ 7th CENTURY B.C.

SCALE OF MILES
0   100   200   300

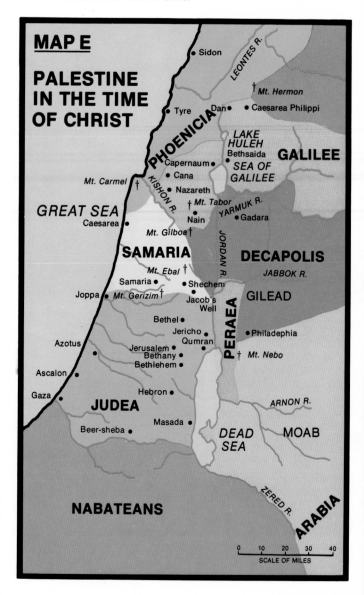

MAP E

PALESTINE
IN THE TIME
OF CHRIST

Sidon •

LEONTES R.

† Mt. Hermon

Tyre •   Dan •   • Caesarea Philippi

PHOENICIA

LAKE
HULEH
Bethsaida
•

GALILEE

Capernaum •
• Cana

SEA OF
GALILEE

Mt. Carmel †

KISHON R.

Nazareth •

GREAT SEA

Caesarea •

† Mt. Tabor

Nain •

YARMUK R.

• Gadara

Mt. Gilboa †

SAMARIA

JORDAN R.

DECAPOLIS

Mt. Ebal †

JABBOK R.

Samaria •

• Shechem

Joppa • Mt. Gerizim †

Jacob's
Well

GILEAD

Bethel •

PERAEA

Jericho •

Azotus
•

Jerusalem •
Bethany •
Bethlehem •

Qumran •

• Philadephia

† Mt. Nebo

Ascalon •

Gaza •

JUDEA

Hebron •

ARNON R.

Masada •

Beer-sheba •

DEAD
SEA

MOAB

NABATEANS

ZERED R.

ARABIA

0   10   20   30   40
SCALE OF MILES

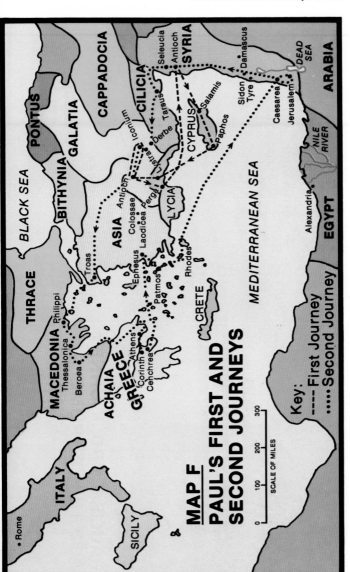

MAP F
PAUL'S FIRST AND SECOND JOURNEYS

Key:
--- First Journey
..... Second Journey

SCALE OF MILES
0   100   200   300

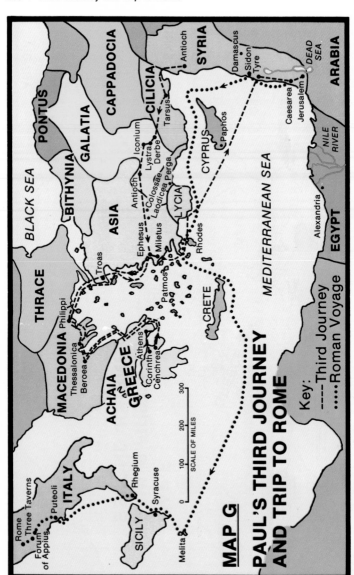

MAP G

PAUL'S THIRD JOURNEY
AND TRIP TO ROME

Key:
---- Third Journey
••••• Roman Voyage